Spiritland

Spiritland

Ghosts of California's Central Coast

Avia Belle Moon

Schiffer Publishing Ltd®

4880 Lower Valley Road, Atglen, Pennsylvania 19310

DEDICATION

This book is dedicated to all the spirits who roam this world. May you find eternal happiness, wherever you are...

Cover photo for Spiritland: California Central Coast satellite image of smoke in the shape of a wolf. The red dots represent the flames of California wild fires, but here they look like the red claws of the Indian wolf spirit. *Courtesy of NASA.*[1] *Copyright 2010. All rights reserved.*

Schiffer Books are available at special discounts for bulk purchases for sales promotions or premiums. Special editions, including personalized covers, corporate imprints, and excerpts can be created in large quantities for special needs. For more information contact the publisher:

Published by Schiffer Publishing Ltd.
4880 Lower Valley Road
Atglen, PA 19310
Phone: (610) 593-1777; Fax: (610) 593-2002
E-mail: Info@schifferbooks.com

For the largest selection of fine reference books on this and related subjects, please visit our website at **www.schifferbooks.com**
We are always looking for people to write books on new and related subjects.
If you have an idea for a book please contact us at the above address.

This book may be purchased from the publisher.
Include $5.00 for shipping.
Please try your bookstore first.
You may write for a free catalog.

In Europe, Schiffer books are distributed by
Bushwood Books
6 Marksbury Ave.
Kew Gardens
Surrey TW9 4JF England
Phone: 44 (0) 20 8392-8585; Fax: 44 (0) 20 8392-9876
E-mail: info@bushwoodbooks.co.uk
Website: www.bushwoodbooks.co.uk

Text and photos by author unless otherwise noted

Library of Congress Control Number: 2011929857

Designed by Mark David Bowyer
Type set in Hurry Up / Zurich BT

ISBN: 978-0-7643-3901-1
Printed in China

CONTENTS

FOREWORD
BY RICHARD SENATE

Avia Belle Moon has penned a unique look at the supernatural side of California's mysterious Central Coast. Much of it is from the mystic view of the Chumash Native American Indians, a people who have long inhabited this area. They see beyond the moving surf and the lonely valleys, and into the spiritual side of the world; they truly move in two worlds—the world of the now, and the world of the supernatural. This book is a deeply personal work that is a journey of understanding and discovery, as Ms. Moon documents her quest for the wonders of the paranormal. It will carry you along as she examines the many ghosts of the Old Spanish Mission La Purísima, a spot where Chumash and Europeans once fought, and where the terrible scars of that conflict remain to this very day. She looks into the haunted halls of the old Santa Maria Inn; here the Hollywood stars of yesteryear may still make an appearance to visitors who open themselves to such things. Her journey takes her to ghost towns, schools, inns, and historic adobes.

I recommend this book for any and all would-be ghost hunters, or travelers with a desire to explore more than what is in the official tour books or Chamber of Commerce tract. You may well discover that you too will be on a quest that might bring new understanding and enlightenment to your own views on this life and the next.

~Richard Senate
Author of *The Ghosts of the California Missions*

INTRODUCTION

When we hear the word "paranormal," several images may come to mind, many of them filtered through the mass media of the Internet, films, and paranormal reality shows. EMF detectors, digital recorders, heat sensing devices, and motion detectors have all become standard equipment for ghost hunters. In recent years, the paranormal has been largely viewed through a scientific lens. When we hear the term "spirituality," the view becomes more abstract and diffuse. We find ourselves looking through a softer lens. I believe for a correct view of death we need both of these "lenses." Paranormal investigation provides us with the scientific evidence to prove the existence of an afterlife, while the spiritual realm allows us to connect with the thoughts, feelings, and emotions of the spirits with whom we are trying to communicate. When both of these "lenses" are in place, a new vision emerges—the para spiritual view.

The first footprints on the virgin soil of the California Central Coast were taken by the Chumash Indians, followed by the Spanish Conquistadors. The legacy of these two cultures left a vast set of "emotional footprints," otherwise known as "ghosts" or "spirits," thus leaving a blueprint in the California earth. The coastline became a land of spirits, destined to roam the earth, skies, and the sea.

When H.L. Williams arrived in Santa Barbara in the early 1900s to colonize the first spiritualist colony, he called his parcel by the sea "Summerland," which means "paradise or utopia" in the Wicca tradition. The Spiritualists practiced mediumship, or the ability to communicate with the dead, thus opening up a world of communication with past spirits. The Spiritualists may well have been the forerunners of a new science for the twenty-first century para-spirituality.

If ghosts can be defined as emotional footprints, then the idea of death becomes secondary, because we all experience times of great emotion. Paranormal research indicates that there are many "ghosts" of people still walking the earth. These are the people who experienced great trauma in this lifetime, leaving behind an emotional footprint on the universal psyche. Thus, "Spiritland" is filled with the spirits of both the dead and alive.

My intent in writing this book is to show that death is not a final destination, but the next stage in the journey of eternal life. I'd like to remove the element of fear associated with ghosts, and to look at them through a new lens, not as something to fear, but as Richard Senate puts it, as "harbingers of hope" for those who are grieving over lost loved ones.

A lifetime of love does not disappear with death, but enters another dimension. The body may disappear, but the spirit does not. When I walk into a room that has the presence of a spirit, I immediately feel its presence. To the visible eye, the California Central Coast speaks of the sun and the sea, yet another world exists that cannot be seen with the eyes, but felt with the heart. This is Spiritland.

~Avia Belle Moon

CHAPTER ONE

THE CHUMASH INDIANS AS PIONEERS OF THE LAST FRONTIER DEATH

What is death? This question still remains unanswered in the twenty-first century. Although science has developed the capability to explore different regions of the universe and return with data that can offer insights into the possibility of life on other planets, we are still unable to determine what happens after we die. As science is still unable to answer the question of death, the term *paranormal* was born, designating experiences that lie outside the range of normal experience or scientific explanation. Beyond the boundaries of conventional science lies the unexplored frontier of the "new sciences," which may include parapsychology, the paranormal, the theories of parallel or interdimensional universes, and another realm, para spirituality, which combines paranormal phenomena and spirituality.

THE CALIFORNIA CENTRAL COAST

The light looked like around 6:30PM. I felt the cool air on my skin, and inhaled the sea, sun, and salt. As I watched a bank of pinkish-gray clouds hanging on the horizon, a seagull skimmed across the olive green waves, soaring through the blare of a foghorn. The sands of time were half in shadow, half in light. Darkness slowly enveloped the beach, as another world emerged…

Through the setting sun, a city of light sits in silhouette. With the rising fog, trees become shadows of silence. The branches tremble, breathing in the fog.

Around 7PM the city disappears and a new land emerges...

This is Spiritland, where lost souls roam the earth, sea, and sky... this particular parcel of the planet is a spiritual vortex of energy, and home to the oldest civilization in North America, the Chumash Indians, said to have inhabited the continent at least 10,000 years ago.[2] A Chumash native says,

> America is called "Turtle Island" by most native people. A NASA image from space reveals a continent that looks like the back of a turtle. "We are at the tip of the tail, or the "Western Gate," where the sun sets. Where the sun rises in the east is called the "Eastern Gate," and then you have a southern and northern gate, so the natives at these gates are in charge of opening and closing these gates. Where the sun rises is the Eastern Gate, allowing new life to enter Turtle Island. In Santa Barbara we are right on the top of the Western Gate, which is the western doorway to the other side, or Shimilaqsha, the Chumash realm of the dead.

The California frontier extended from the Oregon border in the north to the Tehachapi Mountains in the south. Chumash territory extended along the southern California coast from Malibu to some point north of San Luis Obispo, with the densest population along the coast south of Point Conceptión. This area also included the Santa Barbara Channel Islands.

Within this vast territory lies the legend of the Western Gate, which is believed to have originated in Chumash coastal villages along the Central Coast. Some factions in the contemporary Chumash community believe Point Conceptión to be the portal to the next life in North America, and that spirits must pass through the Western Gate to get to this "other side," or Shimilaqsha. The spirits must first undertake a journey commencing at Humqaq, or Point Conceptión, to reach a new dimension of life. This journey actually begins at the time of death, where the spirit undergoes a series of rituals and ceremony to prepare for the journey to Humqaq.

Point Conceptión. *Courtesy of Bruce Hamilton. Copyright 2010.*

A Chumash Elder from the Santa Ynez reservation describes the process:

> When somebody passed away, the women were the undertakers. They prepared and carried the body, and I know when my grandma died, she was 97 years old. We did the cultural way of the Chumash, and that was to get a sheet and sew flowers all around it, and you put it over the coffin. That's what the Chumash used to do. This is what our grandmother, Maria Solares, said. In funerals nowadays a lot of them do mariachis, etc. The Mexican culture was embedded in us. When I go, I want the Indian traditional ceremony, the sheet with flowers. I want the traditional Indian burial. I noticed that at a lot of funerals on the rez, they keep the bodies in the house. It doesn't go anywhere. I put my mother in the tribal hall. I don't believe in showing her in the casket. We did that for my grandma, put roses around the sheet and it felt good, that one touch of culture. I do know that the body was prepared and buried under cactus, so the animals didn't hurt them, with all their belongings.
>
> This whole damn land was reservation. When the Europeans came here they said, "I want that piece of land. It's under the shade, it's next to the ocean, or whatever." Indians didn't think they really owned anything.
>
> How can you buy or sell the sky, the warmth of the land? The idea is strange to us. If we do not own the freshness of the air and sparkle of the water, how can you buy them?

Such was Chief Seattle of the Suquamish tribe's reply to the United States Government, when in 1854, they offered to buy two million acres of land occupied by native people in the Northwest.[3]

A daughter of the Chumash tribe shared her own recollections of burials during her childhood:

> They do believe from the day of the death to the following year to that day, that they also hold another ceremony, but within that time period they believe that spirit or soul during that time period is traveling the earth to every place it's ever gone, like a farewell? And the last ceremony that we do is kind of like our farewell to the soul.

The last ceremony is more for just the immediate family. There are a few items that we save that belong to that individual. The immediate family meets at the campfire they kept going for that person. They rekindle it and get it going, and then they take some of the person's items and throw them in the fire, along with some other things and they say their farewell and prayers, and it's kind of like us letting them know that it's our time to let you go, as well as your time to go ahead and be on your own and make peace.

Santa Ynez.

Her mother shared their own history of Chumash death rituals.

When someone passes from here they put flags at half masts. When somebody died they would bring them into the home and put a sheet and prepare all these little flowers, and while they were doing that they reminisce and tell different stories. I remembered a man started the fire, and the fire kept going until the day the person was buried. We had sage, and we wrapped it as an offering. We burned some sage and cedar grass to purify. They usually have a wake. Real flowers were put on the sheet.

She shared not only the journey at death, but also of the journey she undertook at birth in search of her true Native American roots.

I have a Spanish name. The Indians would take Spanish surnames. My grandpa was from Tucson. I tracked him back to the Yacqui tribe. I went to that area and met a man in the office who was the vice chairman. He said he would introduce me to different people. There are eleven tribes or districts. So he took me around, and the last lady he took me to was 94 years old. They talked in their own language, then we went back to his office and he said "From what I've heard you're from around here." All I told him was that my grandpa left here and went to California. His father's name was C [name protected], and that's all I had to go on, so he told this to the old woman, and then we drove out and she showed me a wash bin and said "This is where your grandfather lived."

It was said that the spirit of the dead before leaving for *Shimilaqsha* went to Point Conceptión. That was a wild, stormy place, and there were no rancherias there. It was called *Humqaq*. There, below the sea cliff in a place which can be reached by lowering a man by a rope down the sea cliff from above, is a pool of water, like a basin—water, fresh water, keeps dripping down from above. And there on the surface of the stone beside the pool of water are footprints of women and children to be seen. There the spirit of the dead bathes and paints itself, and then it sees a light to the westward and goes towards it and thus reaches the land of *Shimilaqsha*, going through the air-not through the water. [4]

SHIMILAQSHA

A PORTAL TO LIFE IN NORTH AMERICA OR MERE LEGEND?

This "other side, *Shimilaqsha*," is not heaven or hell, just another dimension. A living, breathing, existing dimension," says a Chumash native.

In native culture there is no death, just a changing of worlds, so we change from this world to the next world. We don't have a heaven and a hell. The worst things we have on the way to *Shimilaqsha* are the trials that we have to face.

After crossing the sea, the soul first reached the Land of Widows. Women who remained young by dipping themselves in a spring. Past them is a canyon through which the souls must pass with two giant ravens perched on opposite sides that peck out the eyes of the soul as it passes. The soul replaces its eyes with two poppies and restores its sight. Beyond the canyon, the soul encounters a woman with a stinging tail called *La Tonadora.* She kills living persons who attempt to pass, but only annoys souls. Then the soul reaches a shoreline where there are "condemned persons" who have fumed to stone, including "women who knew the mysteries of yerbas." Also on this shore is the *palo,* the rising and falling pole which provides the bridge to *Shimilaqsha*. In the water are people who are "undergoing penance," who fell off the *palo,* and whose lower bodies have been transformed into those of turtles, lizards, frogs, snakes, and fish that must crawl from the water to eat cacomites (bulbs). The soul crosses the *palo* to "a good country" where two roads lead away in separate directions.[5]

THE LIQUID DIMENSION

A Chumash native says:

One of the first things that happens is that a crow pecks out our eyes and they're replaced with abalone, and the reason for that is that in the next dimension these eyes don't work, but those do. I believe it has to do with the fact that we come from the ocean. In fact, everyone comes from the ocean. Our bodies are mostly water. The first life crawled from the ocean. We travel back to this liquid form, into this liquid dimension.

There are unlimited dimensions. We are thinking along our own plane, and we are limited as human beings in our ability to think beyond this dimension. Beginning with the origin of time, that time does not even exist, and Einstein proved that. In our culture, nothing is impossible, and there is no limit. There are other ways to get to the other side in ceremony. In the sweat lodge the air that you're breathing is liquid air. You're breathing steam. It's almost like traveling back into the womb, because in the womb we breathe liquid. I know it's hard to conceive in this dimension, because today we're used to breathing air, but originally we breathed liquid.

Chumash Indian tribe member wearing coyote headdress with abalone eyes.

All cultures have a series of trials they must go through to get to the other side. In Chumash mythology the same thing exists. There are a series of trials that are very difficult. Once you're on the other side it's very difficult to come back. It's not difficult to contact those on the other side. I talk to spirits all the time and they talk audibly, or sometimes through thought and emotion.

The spirits that we find on this side are spirits who have not found their way to the other side. Some of them know this and some of them don't. The majority of them don't know this. It's said that when a person crosses over due to tragedy or during a time of duress, that unless you are escorted to the other side, it is very common for your essence or your spirit to stay on this side, and that's where we get "hauntings" from. "Haunting" expresses an idea we can express readily; for lack of a better term I use this word. We're scared of this entity, and so we consider it to be a haunting. In actuality it's not. It's almost like a big, huge, ugly troll who has no friends. He could be the nicest troll in the world, but every time he approaches a villager they run away screaming. All he wants is a friend. He wants someone to help him on his journey. It's the same thing with the spiritual entities. Some of them just need some help, but when they approach us the living with that closed mentality, we often have the intent to run away screaming. Not us Indians. We have songs, we have ways, rituals, to help these people across, or animals or rock spirits, tree spirits.

SHADOW AND LIGHT IN SANTA BARBARA'S TRAGIC PAST

"Spirits have a tendency to stay where tragedy has occurred. There has been a tremendous amount of tragedy," says the Chumash native. He continues:

> Genocide was practiced here, and infanticide—the Chumash woman killing themselves and their children so they wouldn't have to grow up under Spanish rule. It was horrible here—torture, disease, murder, rape, child rape. I challenge any of the Franciscan padres to prove to me that the Catholic Church was not molesting boys.

Chumash rock art from Honda Ridge, close to Point Conceptión.
Courtesy of Steward, Copyright 2010.

There are ways to open and close this gate, and the Chumash have always opened and closed this gate for their family members. Their relatives, the groups, the medicine people would get together and sing or perform ceremony and open the Western Gate so that our spirits could cross. There have been circumstances though that did not allow that to happen. Once Catholicism and Christianity was brought here the native religions were automatically banned, so we were not allowed to practice our own spirituality, so there are some Chumash entities left behind, but not very many.

Very few of the hauntings are Chumash. There is only one case of what they believe is a Chumash woman. From the Chumash perspective and I don't want to say "hauntings," it's not actually a haunting, but when the Spanish started arriving here, and were developing the land for their ranches, they started cutting down a very sacred plant to the Chumash, and this particular plant is what we use for our visions and for medicine also, and so one of our medicine people saw this and said, "This plant will be gone if we don't do something." This medicine person went into ceremony and called from the other side the Black Dog, and people today who don't know anything about that story have asked me many times and said, "We were out and we saw this, we saw this big black dog where you would not expect to see a big black dog, and it was pretty scary," and I tell this story that this dog was called forth from the other side. Actually it's a wolf, to protect our plants, and that this is a legitimate Chumash, and I hate to call that a "haunting," but there's a legitimate Chumash haunting right there. And that calling was from the medicine or spirituality of the land itself. You can bury a lot of medicine people in 18,000 years, so medicine people, the Chumash, lived in this area for many thousands of years, lived and died, and then the Spanish came. The experience between the Chumash and the Spanish was a prolific one. There were many deaths at the hands of Spanish soldiers. Many Chumash died, and many Spaniards died.

Before the first Chumash stepped onto this land, Creator said this land is going to be the "Western Gate." This land is already a vortex of spiritual energy. I need a people I can depend upon to be the keepers of this Western Gate. I'm from the medicine family of the Chumash. The dolphin, swordfish, and owl clan. Our oral family history is factual, true, and honorable. The Chumash Indians are the oldest culture ever discovered in North America. Our original home is the Channel Islands. About 100,000 years ago there was much less water. The Chumash are believed to be a Tahitian culture that found its way from Tahiti through Hawaii to Santa Barbara. We have mythology that we are from the Little Dipper. We are a "Mu" culture originating from an ancient oceanic continent called "Lemuria."

MISSION SANTA BARBARA AND LA PURÍSIMA CONCEPCION

HAUNTED OR HOLY?

"Show me a mission that's not haunted."

Chumash Native (CN)

Chumash Indian tribe members at Indian powwow.

"You can't convert anybody against their will. It would be a sin on our part to try to convert somebody that wasn't willing to go through with it."

Santa Barbara Mission Spokesperson (SBMS)

CALIFORNIA HISTORICAL LANDMARK NO. 309—MISSION SANTA BARBARA

Known as the "Queen of the Missions," Mission Santa Barbara was founded by Father Fermin Lasuén, on December 4, 1786. The Indian name for the mission was "Tanayan," the name of a Chumash Ranchiera located in Mission Canyon Creek, and means "rocky." Mission Santa Barbara boasts world-famous twin bell towers, an aqueduct built by the Chumash that is so extraordinary it is still used by the city of Santa Barbara, and a façade that includes pink columns with Ionic capitals. Father Antonio Ripoll, who supervised the construction, copied the design of a temple from a Roman book on architecture written in 27 BCE by Marcus Vitruvius Pollio. The temple was considered by Romans as appropriate for a goddess or a virgin. A statue of St. Barbara, a girl who was supposedly beheaded by her father for following the Christian faith, stands at the top of the façade. Mission Santa Barbara is also said to have its own share of paranormal activity. [6 7 8 9]

In Richard Senate's video, *Ghosts of Mission Santa Barbara*, he discusses a room with statues where visitors have reported feeling unseen hands, cold spots in the small chapel, and an unhappy ghost in the bell tower named Don Francisco, who allegedly jumped off when a younger woman refused his advances. The chapel has its own set of ghosts—one of a woman deep in sorrow over the death of a child, who supposedly was comforted by the presence of a brown-robed friar. Strange EVPs (Electric Voice Phenomena) have been recorded in the jail, and guests have reported seeing orbs all over the mission, shadows in the cemetery, monks praying in the church, and have also heard the Mission bells tolling late at night, when the Mission is closed. [10]

Santa Barbara Mission.

What is the nature of the paranormal activity at Mission Santa Barbara and La Purísima Concepcion? What follows is a dialogue between two cultures that created the twenty-one missions which grace the California landscape.

(CN) We all know as human beings that in order for those bricks to go up, something had to fall, and they weren't put up voluntarily. They were put up under duress and force. All twenty-one missions were put up by Native American *slaves*, and I use the term *slaves* not to get a shock value out of you. That's the proper English term for the people who constructed the missions. They were treated as slaves, and worse than the animals. Actually they were treated worse than the animals on the *rancherias* at the time.

(SBMS) I would say it's just not true. They would consider themselves slaves today of course, but when you talk about those times, going back to the 1700s, everyone was practically a slave. The padres had nothing to eat, they shared all their food with the Native Americans. They tried to get them to raise their own crops, their own food.

(CN) Juan Cabrillo arrived on this edge of the continent in the 1540s. The idea of the Spanish Crown was to come to this continent and involve the Native People in this Spanish Church. The idea was the more converts the Spanish Crown had for the church, the more money it could make. When Columbus arrived we were wearing gold. It meant nothing to us, it was a useless metal. You couldn't hunt with it; you couldn't do anything with it. It had no value. The Chumash greeted the Spanish, listened to their words of God, and felt that maybe this could be something they could add to their medicine without realizing that was not the intent of the Spanish. Their intent was to clean the land and the gold and add the people as converts to the Catholic Church, so that they could just put numbers in a book and say this is how many more converts we have for the Spanish flag. The Chumash who said "I don't wanna convert" were killed. Killed or tortured, so it was not a voluntary conversion. If the missions were really a place of God, why would they need to be so strong, so fortified? They wouldn't need to be. A true house of God could be made of paper. These missions were forts, military strongholds. They were built under the disguise of a mission. The same thing with the bricks and crosses and bells of a mission. It conceals the actual physique of the mission, which is a Spanish military stronghold. That's why there's twenty-one of them, and that's why they're all about a day's walk apart from each other. The intent was to make people think these were houses of worship. In actuality they were military strongholds where the priests and soldiers and everyone lived. There is a guard shack by the mission. This is where if you were coming up the road they would stop you and they would ask your business, and that guard shack became a jail. If you were a Chumash not converted into the mission system you could be arrested and made to convert. If they didn't convert you they could do whatever was necessary to make you convert. There are EVPs (Electronic Voice Phenomena) in the guard shack indicating that people who went in there would be violently pushed around. Now there is no indication as to who is doing the pushing except that they are spirits.

(SBMS) The skull and crossbones on the arches of the cemetery represent death. The Native Americans complained about it, so we took it down and buried the bones and put up a replica, so over the door of the cemetery is just a replica of the skull and crossbones. All the missions had presidios. The presidios were built far away to protect the Indians. The Indians were trained to be soldiers to guard the property, and were the *vaqueros*. The padres had the idea that the land belonged to the Indians, and the soldiers that were here were the Indians.

(CN) Very few of the hauntings are Chumash. There is only one case of what they believe is a Chumash woman. Most of the entities at the mission are not Chumash, they are Spanish. One of the ghosts at the mission is a padre who was killed during the 1830s uprising. A padre who was seen rinsing the blood off his hands in the fountain. The mission had two *lavandarias*, a laundry which is a long stone trough. The Chumash women would do laundry there. During the uprising those woman brought out one of the padres and drowned him there, so the mission disassembled it, and there's no evidence, there's no talk of it, there's none of that. The padres that died there are still walking around. They did not die in a way that welcomed them to the other side, and their lives were not clean lives.

Santa Barbara Mission.

(SBMS) The lavandaria—it's still there. It's this thing about killing the missionaries and the padres because they hated them so much. The only ones that saved the Indians from the government was the padres. You can't convert anybody against their will. It would be a sin on our part to try to convert somebody that wasn't willing to go through with it. It's the same old stories. Those Indian stories keep getting better. By our standards today they would be mistreated. I mean the Spanish soldiers beat their wives. It was a different world they lived in at that time.

(CN) There was another gentleman named Don Francisco who jumped from one of the bell towers, so his entity exists there.

Lavandaria at the Santa Barbara Mission.

(SBMS) Don Francisco—I don't know. This has never been proven. What year was this supposed to have taken place? I've heard of this story of lost love. Is there a date for that?

(CN) We have ways to help each other across. It's the other cultures that are stuck here. If you look at the rose garden at the Mission Santa Barbara, you notice that it sits lower, almost like in a ditch, as opposed to on the ground around it, and the reason for it is that it was the pit where the adobe brick was mixed to make the mission, and so one of the ingredients in that is lye. When the Spanish were either killed or when the Chumash died, either by disease, murder, or suicide, the soldiers, in order to not have to bury them, would just throw them in the lye pit and let them dissolve, but that didn't stop work. The other Chumash had to keep making the brick, and that's why I tell people this mission is very much like the Brooklyn Bridge. The Chumash had to keep making the brick, and that's why I tell people that there are human bodies in the Brooklyn Bridge. The construction workers that fell died up there and construction didn't stop, they just encased them in the existing cement and kept right on working. It was the same thing with the mission except that the bodies dissolved in the lye pits were again scooped into brick and mortar, mud hay, put into brick forms, let to dry, and then put again into the mission.

(SBMS) They had what was called a charnel house in the cemetery. After you were buried for so long they dug you up and put the bones in the carnage house, and sometimes they did add lye to it to make the bones decompose that much faster. No, they had too much respect for the deceased. I made adobes myself, but I don't think we put any Indians in there.

(CN) The last curator went into the pit and started an archaeological dig, and found a weather stone. This weather stone is a crystal that our people would use to do their medicine, and many other spiritual works. Everybody who has touched our weather stone is dead. The last curator died, and the last three ground keepers at the mission all quit because of the spiritual activity that goes on there.

(SBMS) We've got guys here from Mexico doing those gardens every day. The only reason they ever quit is because they're not doing a good enough job.

Tree at the Santa Barbara Mission.

At the Santa Barbara Mission there is a painting of Father Serra and an Indian native with his arm draped over the native boy. File cabinets sit in a solemn line behind the desk.

"The records were all written in Latin. This is about the Indian question," says a spokesperson at Mission Santa Barbara, and continues:

> All these stories get mixed up, like when they say they hated Father Serra so much they cut out his heart when he died. The walls—you hear some of the tourists say, "Well that's where they used to tan the Indians' skin." We skinned the Indians to make lamp shades out of them?? Some of this stuff is made up. Listen to this: This man comes by and says ,"I am a freelance writer. I'm on my way to Oregon where I'm going to cover an AMA convention. He says, "I understand you know something about ghosts." We get into this little talk, and he says, "Could you do something with your hands?" We're out in front of the mission. So then he writes in the caption, "Points to place where he saw ghost." I was pointing at the gift shop!
>
> I came here one night looking for a room. I was just visiting, that's when we had students at the time, and there's one wing over here, and it was dark, and all I saw was this white sheet come flowing down the steps. It went right past me and I was up against the wall. It just passed me right by. I couldn't wait until the next day to ask and I says, "You're not going to believe this, but this is what happened to me last night" and they said, "Oh that's what's his name; he's here from the Camaldolese Hermits near Big Sur. He's taking classes with us to get ordained, and they all wear a white robe with a white hood." When he walked down those steps all I could see was a white sheet, and I'm used to seeing all brown. All of a sudden I see all this white coming down the steps. Well that scared me.
>
> This one fellow claims that when they put in the security system they saw something going on in the main room downstairs here. There's this light that just moves around. There's no reason for it, the lights are out, it's night, two o'clock in the morning. Just a light, they don't know what it is, like a dot of light, a white dot that moves around in the dark, like it's walking back and forth.

A murder occurred at Mission Santa Barbara February 28th, 1896. The Morning Press Santa Barbara reported in its article "An Insane Man's Act," that the "man was a protégé of the Father Superior and staying at the mission," and a "forty-year-old native of Germany who had a maternal aunt who was insane." *The Press* then goes on to report that "Bernard Krusemeyer fancied in his hallucination that he had some great grievance against the Father Superior...and that yesterday morning his mania culminated. He went upstairs to the second floor, waiting for the Father Superior. When the latter came up, and arrived at the sixth step from the top, the maniac stood out and leveling his weapon, fired with great rapidity the entire five charges into the person of his imagined enemy, but real friend. The weapon he used was a British bull-dog, five-chambered revolver." One of the priests heard the shooting and "hurried into the Mission, and there found his Father Superior lying at the bottom of the stairs, while the man who did the deed stood at the top of the steps, looking down, his smoking weapon in his hand."[11] Whether the ghosts of either of the players in this tragedy still haunt the Mission remains a mystery.

"At Mission X we heard footsteps in the attic," says a spokesperson at Mission Santa Barbara. "We needed a lock to go open the attic. It would go: *Thump. Thump. Thump*. They would go over it." (Like they paused before stepping over the cross beam.) We went up there with flashlights and no dust was moved, no footprints. There's dust on the floor and you would have been able to see some kind of movement. Three of us heard someone walking in the attic. It was around suppertime, around 6-7 o'clock. I sent two young men up there with flashlights. It was wide open, end to end. There's no place to hide up there… All I can say is that I thank God that I wake up every day on this side of the grass. I've had my fifteen minutes."

Santa Barbara Mission. Stairs where Father Superior was shot.

Richard Senate, nationally known paranormal expert says,

> The Spanish influence is strong. The goals of the missions were not, as some Yankees believe, to make slaves out of the native people. They wanted to bring them into the Spanish system and religion. They wanted to turn them into a good, exploitable work force. Reduce them to a kind of peasantry. In this they were a success. They gave them Spanish names and introduced them to Spanish ideas and foods and music. They also brought their beliefs in such things as vampires and demons, so many of the native peoples died in them. Thousands died young. They were the scenes of battles as well. So much struggle and pain in them has left a psychic scar. When you visit some of the old missions, you can feel the heavy weight of the past lingering in these old buildings. Maybe it's all the history they have witnessed or the layers of psychic energy they hold. They are really mysterious. Every one of the missions in California and the west has at least one ghost, many have more.[12]

Much of the "struggle and pain" that Senate refers to can be attributed to the introduction of diseases by the Spanish colonists. Scientific studies indicate that Native Americans such as the Chumash Indians of the America did not possess any natural immunities... smallpox, syphilis, diphtheria, and even children's ailments such as chickenpox and measles caused untold suffering and death amongst the Native Americans.

The first expedition known to have contacted the Chumash left the Spanish port of Navidad on June 27, 1542, with a fleet commanded by Juan Rodriguez Cabrillo. The group sailed into Chumash territory, and spent time on the Channel Islands, Santa Barbara, and Point Conceptión, exchanged goods with the Chumash people, and engaged in various forms of contact that provided plenty of opportunities for contagious diseases to be transmitted to the Chumash tribes.[13]

Richard Senate claims to have experienced a retrocognitive event that may lead to a paranormal insight into the nature of the suffering and diseases that the Chumash people experienced during the Mission era. "Once, and only once, did I have something that I now believe was retrocognition happen, and it was at a place where traumatic events have occurred. It happened at the restored Spanish Mission, La Purísima Concepción near Lompoc, California."

CALIFORNIA HISTORICAL LANDMARK NO. 340 MISSION LA PURÍSIMA CONCEPCIÓN

The Spanish priest, Father Presidente Fermin de Lasuen, founded Mission La Purísima Concepción on December 8, 1787. The mission was the eleventh of twenty-one Franciscan Missions founded in California, and has been called by Richard Senate "the most haunted of the missions." It is now a California State Park. In the soldiers' quarters you can hear and smell the squeaking, pungent odor of rawhide. On the sign it reads: "A squad of 5-7 leather jacket soldiers maintains order and protects the mission from outside threats. The soldados de querida were protective coats made from animal hides. Their equipment included lances, swords, flintlock, muskets, and rawhide shields." Squirrels pop in and out of their holes in the dry, dusty landscape. Sheep and goats are kept in the corral. A sign lists that in 1820 there were "9,500 cattle, 12,600 sheep, 1,305 horses, 288 mules, 86 swine, 40 goats, and 15 burros."

Vintage photo of La Purísima Concepción Mission. Vieja. *Courtesy of Mission La Purísima Concepción State Historical Park. Copyright 2010.*

Around 4PM, the ranger walks around with a formidable set of keys to lock up the chambers.

Mission La Purísima Concepción.
Master Keys to the Mission.

"Nine ghosts at least," says Richard Senate, who has conducted paranormal investigations at La Purísima, "I have been there at night and it's spooky. I spent most of one night here doing a TV show. Lots of things went on from doors opening to shadows moving. Lots of music—like flutes and Latin chanting. I saw a ghost dog (a lean Greyhound.) I have gotten EVPs at the missions and lots of orbs. Some of the EVPs I've recorded include:

"Covet each day,"
"La Luz,"
"I am here for you, my son,"
"It is for Love," and
"We are here."[14]

He also recalls a retrocognitive experience at La Purísima.

I have visited the place many times over the years, but only once did I have something like this occur. Since then I have tried to duplicate the event at the site several times, without success. When it happened, I had to wonder if I had just imagined it all. After years of research and reflection, I now believe it was a brief example of retrocognition. I was visiting the restored mission with a group at the time. I left the party and went into the old church. There was no one there. As soon as I entered I felt something was different. It was a sort of uneasiness. I sat on one of the benches in the church and meditated for perhaps three to four minutes. Then, I got up and started to walk down the center of the church. As I drew close to the altar rail, I saw something out of the side of my right eye. I turned my head and saw three figures I had not seen before. They were small in stature, almost the size of children. They were kneeling on the floor. They were wearing rags, and one I recall had a blanket around him. They had long hair that was dirty and stringy that hung down to their shoulders. One of the three, the one closest to me, turned and looked up at me. I saw he had scars and red sores on his face. There was a pleading quality in his expression. I also saw behind them a bright mural painted on the wall. It was red, yellow, and green, depicting a sort of decorative vase and swags of flowers. Then, as quickly as it came, the whole thing vanished and I was once again left in the church with a sick feeling in my stomach. I was positive I saw Native Americans, but my vision was nothing like the paintings and depictions of the happy, white-clad mission converts found at this mission and in books. The three I saw were starving, sick, dirty, and miserable. The mural I saw was almost garish and nothing like the paintings that now adorn the restored walls.

Mission La Purísima Concepción.

What had I seen? It didn't last long, just a few seconds, but what I saw was detailed and stark. I researched the event and found there were times in the 1820s when the Natives were starved and epidemics of smallpox did take many lives. Once there was even a revolt that took many Native American lives and Spanish as well.

Mission La Purísima Concepción.

A smallpox epidemic in 1844 resulted in a large number of Chumash deaths, particularly at Mission La Purísima, but also in Santa Ynez.[15]

If I had imagined it, why would I not have conjured up something that resembled the stereotypical image of the missions of old California? Why would I have imaged the faces of the Natives marred by pox? Why wouldn't I have come up with a colorful mural and not the simple, muted colors depicted in pictures? Upon reflection I now believe it was an example of retrocognition. I had gotten my wish, and for a few seconds seen the true image of life at the missions. It was a vision that haunts me still. Over the years I have learned that others have seen and heard things at that Mission. Maybe, like

Gettysburg, this place that witnessed tragedy is somehow scared and when conditions are just right, the past and present dissolve into one.[16]

Mission La Purísima Concepción and Colonel Tapia

A docent at Mission La Purísima Concepción shares his story:

I have been doing Living History reenactments for about eighteen years now. I'm lucky; I get to portray a soldier who was here at the mission at the time. He was the corporal of the guard, and his name was Tapia. He was born in Mission San Luis Obispo, and he was here until about 1824 when they had the revolt. I know where his land grant is, I know who his parents were. His wife, his daughter, everything about him. I can trace his family history back as far as I can my own...

Mission La Purísima Concepción.

He was a very likeable person. If we had met, we probably would have been good friends. When I read about him, and the things he liked to do, hunting and fishing, I think we would have been good friends. He considered himself a Californian. He didn't really have that many ties to Mexico, so he didn't really consider himself to be a Spaniard. He didn't consider himself to be from Mexico. He was a Californian.

His land grant was Rancho Cucamanga, Altura, and Upland, in Los Angeles County, and so he became a very prosperous person. He helped a lot of people keep their land grants when Fremont came through, so we're just very happy that we found him in our archives. We've been able to trace his history and do the reenactments. Tried to do his side of the story and the Indians side without taking sides. I also do a ship captain, but Corporal Tapia is my primary person. I can identify with him because I know so much about him. You have to go through a lot of information and through a lot different channels to get any information from the Catholic Church and the diocese.

We're still researching him, and occasionally we find out new things about him. His land grant, who his daughter was, what they sold the property for. I haven't found out about his death; I understand it was sometime after Freemont came through. Maybe the people in Rancho Cucamanga could find out about it and send me a letter. Everybody says our mission is haunted. I suppose if you believe in ghosts you might see something. In 2007, we were doing a tour. We were inside the soldiers' quarters. The main body of the church is called the quartel. It's the unmarried soldiers' quarters.

In the springtime, probably around May, we were explaining to a group about the muskets. I was explaining about Tapia's land grant, and one of the things it says is that he buried a cache of gold and died before it got dug up, when Fremont came through, and I made the comment that maybe he would come back and tell me where the gold was, and something hit me in the shoulders. It actually hit me hard enough, that I turned around and said "What?" because I thought it was my partner telling me it was lunchtime; there was nobody there.

The young group of people I was talking to all left. A group of teenagers, about 15-16. There was probably ten or twelve of them in there. My partner was like "What are you doing?" and I said "Something hit me." That was all there was to it. It was probably around 11:15 or 11:30AM, and we had just started the program like we did today. We normally have lunch at around twelve. One will go and the other keeps the soldiers' quarters open, and he'll come back, and the other one will go to lunch, so I just thought he had gone to lunch.

A lot of people are superstitious. There are people here in the valley who won't go in some of the rooms. A lot of people have said that they hear voices. They've heard people crying. We've never heard anything like that. I was explaining about my character Tapia. At that time, he was unmarried. He was the corporal, so he had the apartment next door to the unmarried soldiers' quarters. When I read the history book in Bancroft, it talked about his sense of humor and the fact that he had buried a cache of gold. He was born in this area so he understood the Indians better. He was more lighthearted towards them. He wasn't somebody who was angry at having to be here with... I think he grew up with a lot of the Indians. I grew up here in this area, and I know a lot of Chumash. We went to school together. At that time they wouldn't tell you they were Indian or anything because of the hardships. It's gone on in the country for a long, long time. The way they were treated, the reservation life, the broken promises by the American government. Maybe they were ashamed of their own heritage, and that's a terrible thing.

He had gone to the point where he had elevated some of the soldiers here, or some of the Indians to be in our soldiers' outfit. That says a lot about how much he respected and trusted them. He was educated enough. When the Americans came, a lot of unscrupulous things went on. A lot of stealing of property, and stealing land grants from the Indians by the American people. He had the education to go to court and say his peace in front of the American judges and protect land grants. Again that speaks very well of him. He wasn't somebody who was taken advantage of. He helped a lot of people. There have been several things written about him.

Yeah, it was kind of like, "You're going someplace you shouldn't" or "Don't tell that story again," or "I'm here more than you think I am." That was the kind of thing I felt. It wasn't hard enough like he was angry. It was just like somebody would walk up and smack you on the back like as a friend. It was just enough to get my attention, and that there was somebody here with you, so be careful. "Don't joke about me. I'm here more than you think I am." I had just got done telling them. The group was all in front of me. I actually turned my body and looked behind me to see if my partner was standing there, and there was nobody there, and then he came through the other door and said, "What's going on?" and I said, "Somebody hit me. I thought it was you." The people I was talking to didn't see anything because they'd actually left the soldiers' quarters. I think they were very superstitious. It was like "We're out of here" and I thought, could it have been something else? And I thought, *No, I was on the inside of the cot, the door couldn't have hit me, there was nothing that could have fallen off the wall and hit me.* There was just no explanation for it. It doesn't bother me, I'm not afraid of it.

Docent at Mission La Purísima Concepción dressed for re-enactment of Colonel Tapia.

People say there are two or three other spirits in there. It doesn't bother me to go into the rooms. You can hear things. Sometimes you'll hear voices and stuff, but I think it's the way the mission is built. There could be people outside and you can actually hear them talking inside the buildings. The way the tiles are, the voices carry.

This room, once in a while, you'll hear chanting in it. Our old visitors' center. Death chants. These buildings were the infirmary buildings, the hospitals. I would guess it was the Indians. I was in there myself looking at the topography map, and I heard just a low chanting. Sometimes we have music in the chapel, so you kind of expected maybe it was a recording. I came outside, I thought that maybe it was coming from our bookstore. I didn't hear anything up there; it was for just a short period of time. It was just like you heard it. At first I thought that maybe it was a tape recording they were playing for the visitors to hear, but then I've never heard it again so... It sounded like it was a male person. One voice, a lower speaking voice than us. We know that several people died here at the mission. It's well documented, from measles and stuff like that. We have two or three burial sites on the mission property so...those times were no different from today. People live and die every single day, but the hardships. Dying from measles and things that nowadays people are vaccinated for took a heavy toll. I think that almost one time we lost one hundred and fifty people here to measles epidemics. I would imagine a lot of that kind of stuff went on. I've never felt I was threatened by anything out here.

I think anybody can say you'll be walking along, and just out of the corner of your eye you think that you can see something moving, and you look and there's nothing there. That happens here almost all the time. We have the bare bars and the shutters on the windows. The wind blows pretty much all the time. You can be walking around and a shutter will move or something just enough to catch your attention. Again you'll hear the wind blowing through the tiles or the trees and stuff. Sometimes it'll sound like a whistle.

If you look behind the light post at the furthest point, that's called Tranquillion Peak. This is where the Indians here believed you entered and left this planet. You went from the upper world to this world and back. From the underworld to this world to the upper world and

Alul-Tranquillion Peak. *Courtesy of Steward. Copyright 2010.*

back. The whole coastline is very sacred to them. Point Conceptión and Point Arguello, Purísima Point. It's rough. It's called the "Jaws of Honda." It's the roughest sea in California, the graveyard of a lot of ships, but to them it was very sacred.

CHAPTER TWO

THE PARANORMAL ACTIVITY OF SANTA BARBARA COUNTY

THE GAVIOTA COASTLINE

SPIRITS OF THE SEA

The Gaviota Coastline is a stunning expanse of sea, salt marshes, coastal terraces, estuaries, and rocky dunes, spanning seventy-six miles from Coal Oil Point in Goleta to Point Sal near Lompoc. It was the Spanish who coined the name "Gaviota" which means seagull, when they settled in 1769. Prior to the Spanish were the Chumash Indians, dating back thousands of years. Legend has it that they made their way from the Channel Islands via the Rainbow Bridge. Hutash, the Earth Goddess, created a "very long, very high rainbow, which stretched from the tallest mountain on Santa Cruz Island all the way to the tall mountains near Carpinteria." The Gaviota Coast became the home for many inland Chumash tribes, who lived peacefully with nature, and embraced a diverse ecosystem that included mountain lions, black bears, golden eagles, southern alligator lizards, the California Condor, the California Brown Pelican, and of course, the seagull.[17]

Seagulls may have flown the entire breadth of the Gaviota Coastline. Soaring over the Pacific Ocean, spanning a wingspan of almost 145 centimeters, the Gaviota Coast is also home to a diverse blend of spirits and ghosts from the time of the Chumash to the days of California's Wild West. A Southern Pacific railroad trestle which sits close to Highway 101 is actually called a "ghost bridge," which "miraculously has withstood earthquakes and numerous natural disasters during its hundred some odd years of existence....ghosts of the bridge may exist in some form. The Ghost Bridge eerily sits near Highway 101 with a backdrop of the blue Pacific Ocean. It is visible only when the brush is cleared from the southbound lanes."[18]

The Gaviota Coastline at sunset.

HASKELL'S BEACH

A CHUMASH PORTAL TO LIFE AND DEATH?

Given that the Gaviota Coast is inherently Chumash territory, it's not surprising that there are several possible portals to life and death in this area. One such possible vortex of energy is Haskell's beach. For many centuries, Haskell's Beach was the site of a major Chumash settlement with villages and cemeteries, containing many Chumash burials.

The Gaviota Coastline at sunset.

Psychic Louella Diamond shared this experience:

About thirty years ago, I went to Haskell's Beach when I was a high school student. We entered a grove. You could hear the wails and howls, even though it was the end of a sycamore grove; it looked like a dark tunnel at the time. I can almost hear the chimes and the Indian things, and the sounds of things clicking in the trees, like beads and wood hitting wood. I can almost see the faces. Like a light indention of their face. I just knew that I was walking through their energy. And I did that once. As soon as I stepped through it was completely quiet, and then I stuck my head in and it was so noisy. I said "I'll never walk through here again." When I looked back it looked like a swirling vortex. The trees were very dark. It defied reality. 3D; like I was in a tunnel, and I could feel the spirits going through me. When I looked again it was a grove of trees. The trees were still howling. They think they're on a journey for rebirth. They must be able to find their way eventually. There are other places, further up the coast. It's a horrible desecration. They're on a journey and they have to go back. I felt as if they were returning to their mother. Whether that could be Point Conceptión or not, I'm not sure.

A Chumash native relates his experience of being caught in a vortex, close to the Music Academy of the West.

Haskell's Beach. *Courtesy of Haskell's Designs. Copyright 2010.*

I came back to Santa Barbara after studying spirituality. As soon as I get out of my car the weather dropped twenty-five degrees. Freezing ice cold. I was walking on the property and I didn't feel good about it. I got to the place where I was going to play my flute. It started to warm up. I started walking towards my car and I could hear a din, almost like people were around me at a distance. It stayed at a distance and then it got louder. It became a murmur, and then a cacophony. Some of them in horror, in anger, afraid. Hundreds of them; then the air began to thicken as if the circle was closing around me. I was running fast by this time. It got to the point where I could physically feel the throng around me. They were yelling in my ear. I could hear hundreds of voices around me. The air was thick. It went up from freezing cold. It was like being at a rock concert. I ran to the car. I was terrified. I haven't been back since.

THE CALIFORNIA STAGECOACH ROUTE

It's 1861, and Mr. and Mrs. Elmer Smith are traveling from Santa Barbara on the California Stagecoach route over the San Marcos Pass to visit Mrs. Smith's sister, Margaret, in San Francisco. The stagecoach turns left off the Pass and onto Stagecoach Road. Mr. Smith appears to be a bit discombobulated. Mrs. Smith turns to him.

"Oh Elmer, whatever is wrong with you? You been twistin' and turnin' in your seat just like a snake in the woods!"

"I reckon if this buggy don't stop in the next ten minutes I'm gonna have to piss right outside this window!"

"Oh Elmer, you're such a child! Can't you wait a few minutes? Look at how lovely it is, with all the oak trees."

The stagecoach makes it way around a bend. Cold Springs Tavern Relay Station appears before them. The coach pulls to a stop and the driver hops out. "We're here folks. Cold Springs Tavern!" He opens the door and holds his hand out to Mrs. Smith. "Let me help you out, ma'am."

Mrs. Smith stands up and tries to get out of the coach. "Why, thank you sir, you are so kind!"

Mr. Smith pushes her aside and jumps out of the coach. "Out of my way darlin', nature's calling!"

Mrs. Smith sighs. "I should have married that fine gentleman from New York. I imagine my life would have been like champagne on ice!"

Wells Fargo Stagecoach Stop #26

The Cold Springs Tavern

On a Sunday afternoon, as you turn off of Stagecoach Road from California Highway 154, it's not unusual to see cars lined up on both sides of the road. As you get closer you can hear *bluesy* music flowing through the oak and sycamore trees. Cold Springs Tavern is on the left. Built in the 1860s by Chinese laborers as a place of rest for stagecoach passengers on the Gaviota/San Marcos Pass, it still remains a favorite for many locals who want to escape the heat of the city and relax in the cool mountain atmosphere. Harley Davidsons are parked in front, gleaming in the late afternoon sunshine. The smell of beer infiltrates into the barbecued beef. A wind comes up the pass and lifts dry leaves into the air, into the smoke rising up from the barbecue, creating an almost supernatural mist. Upon walking into the tavern you can immediately feel a paranormal presence. Could it perhaps be a resident from the buildings of a ghost town at the back of the property, brought in from Gopherville, California?[19]

Spirits have been detected at the Tavern; even on the day of this interview, an EVP was recorded. The chief chef at the tavern shared his experience:

> I've worked here seventeen years. The ghost who I saw walks up the hill past the guy who makes sandwiches, where the jail is. I've seen it probably like three times; usually we see it when it gets dark early; sometimes it gets dark around five or so. We've seen her somewhere around ten or eleven; she looks like she is dressed in the forties, wearing a long white dress. We thought it was a person, but when we looked again, she was gone. The busboy

has seen her too. He doesn't want to do the mats no more because he's seen her a few times. The kitchen mats, floor mats; he cleans them outside the kitchen; that's when he saw her walking up the hill past the jail, here in the back.

The Cold Springs Tavern.

He continues between the harmonica playing in the background, the constantly ringing phone, the "vroom vroom" of a biker revving up his Harley, and the din of people's voices.

> At home I saw a silhouette; not black but kind of smokish. It was like a women's silhouette, like if you're smoking inside and it makes a picture out of smoke; and you look and it kind of disperses into the wall. So what does that mean? Like around 3:30AM. The computer goes on and off. In the middle of the night. And the TV box, when it's red it's off, and green when it's on. We seen it turn green several times. Me and my nephews have seen the ghost. My nephews are terrified of her. I got mad at her and asked her to move, and now she's in their room. At least three times; my nephews have seen it more. I told her she could stay if she was nice, but I didn't want to see her, and said "Go somewhere else." They've seen her in their room. They've seen the smoky silhouette. I never told them anything. Then one day they said, "I gotta tell you something. There's something in my room that's not supposed to be there. I thought I was dreaming but I was wide awake." I never seen something so clearly as her...

At this point, the author caught an EVP on the tape during the interview—an unidentified voice, sounded like something slurping or saying "you."

The Cold Springs Tavern.

Healing Spirits

"One time I got really, really sick," continues the chef.

My mom went to a place called "Campiko." It was an old house with people. They had contact with spirits. They said they would come late at night and take care of me, but they used to come early, like around eleven or twelve; you could nearly feel the pinches of a needle. You know before there used to be a glass, like a bullet? You used to need a small saw to break it. Well, I used to hear that and feel the pinches. I got cured. I still have on my head lots of bumps. Here, feel it.

I got like a lot of scars. But then I got better.

The Cold Springs Tavern.
Photo of author.

Las Cruces

Ghost Town of "The Crosses"

As you walk further inland, the cool sea dissipates into intense dry heat, and you can hear the crunching of your shoes on dry leaves as you walk on trails lined with poison oak. Further inland, close to the Gaviota Tunnel, lies the ghost town of "Las Cruces," or "The Crosses," which was given to a military official named Miguel Cordero, as a Mexican land grant.[20]

The adobe was constructed around 1860. A bridge across Gaviota creek served as a crossing for travelers going to the Gaviota Pass in the 1800s. During this period a barn east of the adobe was built to allow the changing of horse teams for stagecoaches. In 1864, Las Cruces became a stop along the stagecoach route.

From *A History of the Las Cruces Adobe:*

> In those days a stage stop at one's house provided the owner of the house with a substantial income, with the owner providing meals for the travelers and often a night's lodging as well. This, in addition to a crew who boarded full time in order to serve the needs of the coach line, resulted in considerable revenue. The final route approved was to pass by the house of a local sheep rancher, Wilson Corliss. However, his wealth was short lived, as he and his wife, along with a shepherd were found dead a few days after the decision, the structure burned to the ground, resulting in one of the bloodiest murders in the history of Santa Barbara County.[21]

Psychic Louella Diamond shared her own view of what occurred at Las Cruces.

> There was a violent storm here in this river bed. People were swept away. I'm seeing them grabbing onto branches, yelling and going downstream. A horrible storm. I don't know the exact date, but the adobe was fresh looking. I would say between 1890-1930. They were sinners. They were Caucasians. I'm also seeing people

Las Cruces Adobe Ghost Town.

who are lost who are coming for solace. There was some kind of storm—around the turn of the century. Maybe late 1920s. A weather catastrophe, flooding, lightning. Could have been the cause of its end. The feeling was around 1888. At the creek bed. It's eerie, I see a skeleton and bones. The storm was very big and bad. I see people scrambling around down below in the water. The water is high and they can't get it out. It's like a flash flood. At the adobe I can also see a boot ramming through the wood.

Could this have been the boot of Wilson Corliss as he tried to escape his fate at the adobe? Perhaps the answer can only be found in the howling of the wind through the mountains at Gaviota Pass.

Close to the Pacific Ocean lays Ellwood, where the Gaviota Coastline became known for the first Japanese attack on the U.S. mainland by a Japanese Imperial Navy's submarine I-17. In the late 1930s, Kozo Nishino was commander of a Japanese tanker taking on crude oil at the Ellwood oil field. On the way up the path from the beach to a formal ceremony welcoming him and his crew, Nishino slipped and fell into a prickly-pear cactus. Workers on a nearby oil rig broke into guffaws at the sight of the proud commander having cactus spines plucked from his posterior. Then and there, the humiliated Nishino swore to get even.[22]

Las Cruces Adobe Ghost Town.

CALIFORNIA HISTORICAL LANDMARK NO. 361

THE LOBERO THEATRE

"A challenge: Try and find a theater that isn't haunted. Theaters tend to be haunted. There's something about the audience and what the actor is projecting that has something to do with it. These are theories, but not concrete facts. The older the better. I trace it back to Shakespeare's Globe. It goes back four hundred years, the ghost light. Why? I don't know. My friend, a very metaphysical lady and a psychic, said 'Oh, I have the answer—ghosts can now go to the plays because they don't have to buy a ticket."

Richard Senate

The serpent that did sting thy father's life. Now wears his crown. Cut off even in the blossoms of my sin. And each particular hair to stand on end, Like quills upon the fretful porcupine.[23]

Hamlet, ghost scene

In William Shakespeare's *Hamlet*, the ghost of Hamlet's father comes back to tell him that he was poisoned and murdered by his brother, Claudius. Supernatural elements commanded a strong presence in Shakespeare's plays.

Nowadays, ghost lights are left burning in theaters for both practical and perhaps supernatural reasons as well. In the same way that night lights are left glowing in bedrooms all night, the ghost light is left on all night in the theater. It is also believed by some that they may deter ghosts from appearing late at night.

The ghost light was burning on February 22, 1873, an auspicious date in the history of Santa Barbara. That evening was the opening night of the Lobero Opera House, and the culmination of the dream of Giuseppe Lobero, an Italian immigrant from Genoa. The music of Verdi, Rossini, and Donizetti floated off the adobe walls to the *alfarje*, a Moorish ceiling made of inlaid and painted wood. Glowing blood red walls, ethereal light from the magnificent chandelier, and candelabras all fused together to create a mysterious atmosphere of sight and sound.

Ghost Light at the Lobero Theater.

The *Santa Barbara Daily Press* wrote, "We congratulate Senor Lobero on such a monument to his enterprise and love of art, and the town on having such a citizen." We can only imagine "Jose's" excitement as the curtain rose in what was deemed to be his "magnificent temple."[24]

The Lobero Theater.

Nowadays, performances at the Lobero Theater usually begin around 7:30PM, leaving from six to seven a frenzied time when the stage hands are running around taking care of last-minute business. The opening night of a theater performance can be exciting, exhausting, and sometimes frustrating for a stagehand. Their unseen presence and hard work is felt in every aspect of the production, in such tasks as assembling scenery, tying knots, and moving heavy equipment. It was in October of 1998 that an employee at the Lobero Theater felt an unseen presence, and experienced something to which to this day she has difficulty explaining.

The Lobero Theater.

> My husband and I came in the evening, around six. We had turned off the alarm, so we were sure that no one was in the theater. We were under the stage in the basement rummaging through some old costumes when we heard what sounded like a heavy equipment box rolling across the stage. We both looked up to the ceiling and could follow the sound. I thought someone was here, so I went to the stage and called out for the technical director, but no one answered. We went back to what we were doing. Then a few minutes later we heard the same sound going back in the opposite direction. At that point it really freaked us out. I went back upstairs and there was no equipment box or nobody on the stage. When I turned back around my husband was standing at the bottom of the stairs holding a prop spear! I could see he was scared! I said "I think it's time to leave," and so we set the alarm and left. That was that.

Or was it? Over the years, the Lobero has experienced paranormal phenomena that suggests there is a spirit living in the theater by the name of "Harry." In 1977, a stage hand/night watchman named Harry Podea passed away on the premises. He lived and worked at the Lobero for quite a number of years.

> People have heard footsteps walking upstairs in the hall between his former bedroom and the bathroom, lights being turned off and on. Sometimes you can hear running water in the bathroom.

Another employee at the Lobero has had an open door slammed on him. Could it be Harry venting his frustration at the hard, often unrewarded work of the stage hand?

> The evening would have been the time for Harry to be on stage, performing his duties. "As it was rolling across the stage I thought, *That sounds like someone pushing an equipment box.* The only thing I can think of is that it was just Harry going about his work. You know, if someone expended a lot of energy in the theater, why wouldn't they want to stick around?"

Other employees have also had experiences. A manager of the theater was doing laundry in the theater one afternoon. He was alone, except for three people in the box office and a person in the main office. Or was he alone?

> I was loading clothes into the washer when I heard what sounded like footsteps, then a scuffling sound, then footsteps. I kept loading, then came up to the stage to see who was there. It was all dark and no one was there. I went back to the box office and asked and everyone replied they had not gone into the theater. Then I asked the guy in the main office and he said the same thing. There could be no mistaking the sound of footsteps, as they were as clear as a bell. The only thing I could think of was "old building."

The Lobero Theater. *Courtesy of Elisabetta Lucernari*

Santa Barbara has its share of theaters that have experienced paranormal activities. A theater projectionist who has worked in Santa Barbara since 1979 has his own share of paranormal theater lore.

> I went to the X Theater to run a film, and when I arrived, I got the movie ready, and when I went to start it, the lamp won't light. If you don't have a lamp, you don't have a picture. I checked everything and everything was fine. All the circuit breakers were on, so I said, "Okay, I'll look into this later." I went to the second projector as a backup, started it and it ran fine. When I went back to the first projector to see what was wrong, the lamp lit right up. And I told the manager about it, and she said, "You didn't say 'Hello Booth.'" And so from then on, I started saying "Hello" when I went into the projection room and everything worked fine.
>
> I believe it might be the old stage manager, the projectionist also. He committed suicide, and it might be his ghost. She just said, "You didn't say 'Hello' when you went in there, and so the ghost was mad," and so he was playing with me or something. I knew the old stage manager. He used to work at a mortuary as an embalmer, and he was an embalmer in Vietnam. When he got out he came to Santa Barbara and he was working at a mortuary, I forgot which one, and he did projection work as a side job. I checked the circuit breakers, I checked the big circuit breakers, and everything was on. When I came back to it after I looked at the second projector, it lit right up.
>
> We had a guy who used to work here. He was a projectionist and a manager, and he did the same job I did; he used to go around and fix things. One year he was here for the Film Festival, and one of the dimmers that makes the lights go up and down was not working in the theater, so he said, "I know where there's a spare part," so he went to the XX Theater and into the projection room, and two hours later he hadn't gotten back yet. Now the manager who is currently working here went to look for him. Found him dead in the projection room, lying on the floor, dead of a heart attack. Later, a friend of mine was working on some stuff, and he said he saw this figure appear, and the figure walked down and he just disappeared into the stairs. And he asked what does my friend look like? And I explained what he looked like and he said, "That's what he looked like, like it was a silhouette." He didn't see a face, just a silhouette. He tells that story now.

LA CUMBRE JUNIOR HIGH SCHOOL

THE FINAL ACT

La Cumbre Junior High School is Santa Barbara's oldest intermediate school. It was designed in 1926 and opened in 1928 as a junior high school serving grades seven through nine. Unique to this campus is a mural that graces the cafeteria, a gift to La Cumbre by the art students of 1986. The Spanish-style school is housed on a 21.95-acre campus on the west side of Santa Barbara. The mural depicts the past, present, and future of the Santa Barbara community. [25]

The beat of "Thriller" pounded through the La Cumbre Junior School as they rehearsed for their upcoming musical review in January. An employee at the theater shared his own experience of the paranormal activity present in the theater.

> It's an old theatre. I know that somebody supposedly died here. His name was Edwin. It was when they used to use sandbags for counter weights. Now they use steel. You have a fly system. The more weight you put on the banisters; they just counter weight the fly system. I fly in a door. I need to counter weight. Sandbags are about 100 to 400 pounds. One little counter weight is 30 to 50 pounds. The rope probably got worn, snapped, and fell… He died in the 50s. I don't know. Maybe the light heated up the rope and it broke and the sandbag fell. The kids know about this—they all wanna know, is it true? I was thinking that he would be happy that we're doing things here again. I didn't care if it was haunted or not.
>
> When I came in a couple times on Monday, every light—and when I say every light, I'm gonna show you what I mean—I came in and all of the lights in the theatre were on, and the thing is that the computer was off. To turn it off, I go report, exit, shut down, and that's how you control it from here, and the thing is, it's happened twice, and I can't explain it. It turns everything on. Once you turn this on, you control everything from here.

There are one-two hundred lights. They were just all on. You have to push this button, and this turns this on, but this wasn't turned on. I had people come from downtown, because if the lights were on at full blast, something could have burned. You get 50,000 watts of light and it gets really hot. Those are the two big things. I feel his presence. And ever since then—always it's right over here, and there's nobody there. I used to come in here like on the weekend and it would be all dark. It's a little spooky. You look and you'll see this outline of something. I called the people in New York and there's no explaining it. It happened two years ago. We still have the same wooden seats they put in 1927. It's a historical landmark, the whole school.

La Cumbre Junior High School Theater.

He died on the stage. Like yesterday the girl I was talking to said, "Oh, I'm talking to Edwin." They all know about him. These kids mess with him all the time, and maybe Edwin may think that he is one of the kids. And he messes around like these kids do, turning on the lights, etc. Then the paranormal makes sense.

Members of the stage crew are not the only employees at La Cumbre Junior High who have experienced paranormal activity. A maintenance man has also had a strange experience.

> Well, I was taking my lunch around eight o'clock at night, four years ago. I was watching TV, and suddenly the volume starts going up and down. What I noticed was the lines from the TV. The lines were going up and down, and then the TV turned off by itself and I had the control by my side, so I wasn't touching it. This was Room 111. I was watching the lines go up and down. I was the night supervisor at the time.

SUMMERLAND

HOME OF THE SPIRITUALISTS

A painting of Summerland sighs of a wind blowing across a sea dotted with white sailboats. A strip of beach stretching into a faraway mountain. California poppies dot the iceberg lettuce lining driveways in the hills. The streets of San Francisco run through Summerland. Streets lined with two-story blue-gray houses hidden by bougainvillea. A white steeple soars into the clouds above a stained glass window of praying hands. Shops selling oriental rugs, day spas, antique stores, and art galleries line the main street. You can smell the sea through the din of the cars rushing by. Above it all, an American flag ripples into the searing blue sky.

On the outskirts of the city, white horses graze beside a quiet rustic road lined with white birch trees and bird of paradise flowers. A huge tree sits alongside the road that looks like a deer with its legs tucked underneath it. A squirrel runs into a hollow in the tree, while a cloud of dust from a tractor hangs on the road.

Summerland is the first place in the world to have offshore oil drilling, and has some of the most expensive real estate in the world. In 1889 it also became a center for the Spiritualist Church.

Excerpt from letter written from Summerland founder, H. L. Williams, on September 24, 1892:

> "To make Summerland what it was intended by the spirit world—to be a beacon light for the world, and to serve the undoubted and immense mineral resources of the Ortega Rancho for the benefit of and to aid the promulgation of the truths of Spiritualism...to build homes for worn out mediums, sanitariums, colleges...to aid in the most practical way, the higher classes of mediumship."

Summerland Beach.

The Spiritualists believe there "is a sixth sense that develops in some people, an awareness that enables communication with spirits of the dead and with each other." Séances were gatherings of Spiritualists to communicate with spirits, and were conducted by mediums or simply a group of believers. They were conducted in Summerland, in which "believers saw buglers, ghosts, a seven-foot-tall black man, and a naked cherubic child about two and half feet tall with golden curls. [26]

The Spirit of the Big Yellow House is a book written by Rod Lathim that chronicles the history of Summerland and its founding family.

> The transcendentalists came in the 1900s from the East Coast, so that before they came there was a lot of life and death here. The

Big Yellow House was built by Williams. He owned Ortega Rancho and Ortega Hill. The man who owned the white peaked house on Ortega Hill was the founder of Yosemite Park—Galen Clark. These transcendentalists that started coming out to the Santa Barbara area had originally started sending their family members out to California to actually get sober, and as these people grew in their sobriety they were writing letters to the East Coast telling how nice it is out here, so more and more people started coming out here, and so more and more people started moving to Summerland. At the time it wasn't called Summerland. Summerland was a name that Williams picked.

Summerland is described by the Wiccans as a place of peace and paradise that all spirits go after death to rest before their next incarnation.

THE BIG YELLOW HOUSE

One of the most famous landmarks of Summerland is "The Big Yellow House," originally built by H.L. Williams, which in more current times was said to be haunted by several spirits, including a boy named "Hector." Rod Lathim managed the wine cellar of The Big Yellow House in the mid 70s.

The cover of my book has the basement with the stone foundation and the wine cellar. The windows along the front are still there. Above the first floor is a second floor, done after the turn of the century. That was how the house looked like when it was originally built. Hector had youthful energy. He would basically zoom through the rooms. There was a big *L*-shaped long hallway. He would run around the middle table; for me the best way to describe it was the physical sensation. When he was present the air was very thick. It's almost as if someone had sucked the air out of the room and there was pressure on my head, like visually in "Star Trek" when they beam up the silver. Other people can pick up on him sometimes. His energy—there was no question he was a boy. Maybe eight-ten years old. He would always turn off the light on the stairway. I would stand at the bottom of the stairs and say, "You turn that light back on," and it came on. I turned around and it went off, then turned around again and it came on. I would always turn that light on and he would turn it off. He also liked to hide the watering can—the old pewter watering can; it was like a game. It was a very comfortable, playful kind of relationship.

The wall in the cellar looked like it had been plastered over. It was a little bit strange. I think that's where he used to hang out because the energy there was intense. He knew he was welcome here. The spirits felt comfortable at The Big Yellow House. I'd see people upstairs as well. The red room had very weird energy in it. The room was always cold. Things would move—water glasses would move. I use to sit at the top of the stairs on a bench, and it was like there was a party going on up there. I saw the people upstairs in great detail. It was always dark. I saw people, men in dresses, men in tuxes and ties, formal wear, clothing from that period. They never approached or interacted with me. Spirits would come and go. These people were so diverse and varied. It was like sitting in a train station. It didn't feel like they were stuck there or trapped. This area does have a higher frequency of spiritual activity. If you go to Lookout Park, he donated that land so that it could be made into a park. Williams was a good man, and had hopes and dreams for Summerland. When oil was discovered here, the town changed, but before oil was discovered it was a very sweet focused town. The spiritualists were wonderful people.

The Big Yellow House.

The Big Yellow House.

Doorknob on The Big Yellow House.

THE KALEIDOSCOPE INN AND THE SCENT OF SPIRITS

The Kaleidoscope Inn is a restored 1887 Victorian Home in Nipomo built by retired rancher Vitalis Runels. He lived in Nipomo for 40 years and died November 28, 1927. Each window of the house is bordered in stained glass, creating a "kaleidoscope" effect as sunlight streams into the home. Thus the name, "Kaleidoscope Inn." An employee related different stories he has heard from guests and employees who have experienced paranormal activity.

One guest has related how he saw the image of a woman dressed in a robe walk through a closed door, look around the room and sit on the edge of the bed before getting up and walking back through the closed door, never to be seen again. Some guests were staying in the "Lover's Nest," which is one of our rooms in the corner of the house. They left the room and pretty much left the covers rolled up, and just went out to dinner for a couple of hours. No one else had been in the house, and when they came back all the clothes were piled up in the middle, and they thought that was very odd. They asked us the next day if we had gotten into the room and tidied it, and we said, "No," especially not at 8 o'clock at night. That was about three or four years ago; it only happened one time. It was weird enough that they pointed it out to us.

Another experience was about a maid who was with us for a while. She hasn't worked for a couple of years. She used to ask us if we had any kids that lived in the inn, and we said, "No we don't, why?" and she said, "I keep cleaning and hearing laughing and playing in there, and then I'll come back down and see children's footprints on the stairs where I just vacuumed." She said it happened more than once; it happened several times, and she asked, "Are you sure nothing's going on?" and I said, "No, we don't have any kids, and I can't imagine." She said, "There would be footprints on the stairs, and I'm the only one in the house, and I thought that was kind of odd." She said it happened on several occasions. This happened around 2005-ish.

FOOTSTEPS IN THE ATTIC

An employee related different stories he has heard:

We haven't lived there for about four years now, but when we did, there would be instances where we'd be sleeping at night, and it really did sound like someone was walking around the attic, like patterned footsteps, like *creak, creak, creak, creak*. It did seem like it was coming from the attic area above us. We were in the master suite a floor above it, and it sounded like somebody was actually on the floor above us. I got up there once to check, but I never saw or ran into anything. I would go to lie back down and it would start up again, and we did hear that quite often. Footsteps in the attic. The only thing that's happened recently—the Jasmine Retreat on the second floor of the main house. It seems like every once in a while…the last time it happened was like last weekend. The smell of perfume.

The Kaleidoscope Inn.

The Kaleidoscope Inn.

> It's like somebody spilled perfume in there, and the first time it happened was like six-eight months, maybe a year ago. I had to clear everything out, wash everything, clean the carpets, air the windows, and that seemed to clear it out. Then about three weeks ago the same thing happened again. You walk in and the room is clean, it just smells like perfume. The room is clean and orderly, but it smells like perfume, and it's always the same smell, like a women's perfume. We had to clean everything and it's more of a time thing than a clean thing. It happened last weekend again. It's getting to be annoying. We had to clean again, the smell is so strong.

THE SANTA MARIA INN

HAUNT OF THE RICH AND FAMOUS

What do Demi Moore, Clark Gable, Charlie Chaplin, Marilyn Monroe, Rudolph Valentino, Shirley Temple, and John Wayne all have in common? Besides being movie stars, they have all been guests at the Santa Maria Inn. The Santa Maria Inn opened May 16, 1917, with 24 rooms, 24 baths, a kitchen, and a dining room by Frank McCoy, a retired employee of a Union Sugar plant. Two years later, McCoy added 12 more rooms, and in 1923, he added another 21 rooms and a second dining room. Another 28 rooms were added in 1928. During its early years, the Santa Maria Inn began developing a reputation as a place to stay for travelers journeying along El Camino Real. Original guest books in the administration office attest to the inn's famous and not-so-famous visitors. Movie executives made the inn their headquarters while using the Central Coast countryside and oceans as backdrops for films such as *The Ten Commandments*.

The El Camino Real morphed into the present day Highway 101 in 1950. Motorists sped off to newer chain hotels, and the inn eventually closed, not to open its doors again until 1981, undergoing many renovations. Renovations tend to disturb spirits, and since the Santa Maria Inn has reopened there have been ghost sightings and unexplained things that happened in the original parts of the hotel. [27]

The Paranormal Activity of the Santa Maria Inn

In May 2007, the Revenue Manager witnessed his briefcase fall from the chair and roll over end to the middle of the room, standing upright. In the kitchen, after the renovation, the serving trays stacked on a wall shelf began to spin out of control by themselves, suddenly stopping.

The Santa Maria Inn.

A hotel guest staying in the Patio Suites Room was nearly hit by a light bulb shooting out of the fixture above; not a pressure socket but a regular "screw in" type.

Another guest awoke to several silhouettes of people having a party in her room, dressed in mid-1800s-style clothing.

Housekeepers have opened locked doors to find furniture mysteriously stacked in a corner.

Another housekeeper was followed by a balloon as she cleaned the second floor. It then followed her down to the first floor!

Other housekeepers have been touched on the shoulder and were so scared they fled the inn, never to return again, (not even for their paychecks)!

Elevator doors mysteriously open on their own as if waiting for their guests.

A night auditor went to a room to check on a clock that a guest reported wasn't working, only to pick the clock up to see the hands moving forward in an orderly fashion, and stopping at the exact same time of day. Another night auditor has seen the oven door of the kitchen wildly opening and closing as she gets her morning coffee...

The piano in the ballroom has been heard playing by itself.

A housekeeper has heard her name called in the room where Rudolf Valentino stayed, but no one was in the room with her.

At the Santa Maria Inn, "You feel as if you've been transported to another era," (as the room phones recording remind you) as soon as you walk into the main lobby, a paranormal feeling hits you. Frank Sinatra sings "I Believe" as shadows of guests walk past stained glass windows. A tour bus carrying Italian tourists pulls up, and soon the inn is filled with phrases like "Gratzie" and "Ciao."

As soon as you walk into the lobby the feeling of "paranormal" hits you. The elevator door slides open, like a cold metal slab to a morgue. It slides open so slowly, so very creepily. When you enter the room, the first thing you notice is that the clock is off by about forty minutes. Karaoke floats up from the bathroom floor. "The Tracks of My Tears." "Sugar Sugar, Honey Honey." "How Deep is Your Love?" "Fantastic Journey." Easy listening for ghosts.

A brass goose head sticks out of the wall, waiting for a hat. The bathroom, with its whirlpool and fixtures brings to mind the bathtub scene from *The Shining.* The fog outside infiltrates into the room... from the mist materializes the ghost stories of the Santa Maria Inn.

A gentleman was checked into room 132, one of the master suites on the original side; about fifteen minutes later, he came to the front desk, his face pale white. He had no previous knowledge of the paranormal aspects of the Santa Maria Inn; he looked like he had seen a ghost. He asked if there was anything strange about the hotel and the clerk answered that in the past, things had happened in room 221. He said he wanted his money back and left immediately afterwards. He said he had seen a figure of someone in the room. This was about eight o'clock at night.

A maintenance man was painting 221 and found strange marks on the wall. It was weird for him because he had never seen scratch marks or nail marks, like when you have ink underneath your nails and you scratch the wall. They were next to the bed, on the left hand side. He painted over it; that was six months ago.

> I haven't been into the room yet. It was strange to me because I haven't seen it in another room. It was just the prints, and those weren't kids, you can see the mark was from adults, big fingers; could be from a woman or a man, but not from a child. I asked a housekeeper to come in and look, and she ran out of the room. Sometimes you can hear alarms, and the time was changed on the clock. They want you to know they are there. That's what I learned from the TV shows.

One manager has worked there for nine years.

> They have cameras everywhere, and there is one in the wine cellar. I would watch the camera up front and watch the monitor. I could see orbs everywhere, shooting down from the ceiling. I would run down there to see if there was activity, and there's nothing. And sometimes the orb will be in the form of a bubble. Like somebody is actually blowing bubbles from a container, and they'll float everywhere, and I would go down and tell the guests, "Do you know

there are bubbles flying around your head?" and they say, "No." Even though it's dark in the wine cellar it's still lit up, but lately it's been really quiet—no activity—the cameras aren't picking up anything there. No activity.

"Not in that area," says another employee.

I was down in the wine cellar, and the housekeeper had just gone down and was cleaning it to get wine out to stock the bar when all of a sudden I smelled something. I thought it was burning, and it smelled like sulphur; like matches, and it was in one area of the bar, and so I called engineering and when they came in, it disappeared. The smell was gone; that was two and a half weeks ago; it was about 1PM. I usually stock the bar at that time. It felt real heavy in the room. Usually when I go in the wine cellar, the bartenders will get angry at me because I start talking to the ghosts. "It's just me. I just came to get the wine. I've been here for five years, and they would say, "Don't do it," because it sort of freaks them out. One time I didn't do that; it was about a year and two months ago. On the one side is where the white wine is, and there's a separate room for the red wine, and I didn't say, "Hello." I was just doing my thing, and then four bottles just came off the wall and onto the floor and ruined the rug. I ran out of the room. I'm one of those people who wants to see. I want to hear and experience, but it scared me so much I ran out. Twelve bottles came off onto the floor and ruined the rug that was there. I ran out of the room. I do not walk into that wine cellar without saying, "Hello." The one time I did not do that, I had twelve bottles of wine fall off. I heard it and saw them falling and ran out of the room. I have a conversation, and it's never happened after that. That's all they want, friendliness.

In the nine years that I've been here, I've had several different bartenders down there. One bartender said she was doing her paperwork when something told her to look up, something told her to turn her head, and the chair at one of the tables was rattling back and forth, and she told them, "When you're done, clean up your mess and turn off the music."

We had one group that I took to the wine cellar, and that's when I believed they had their cameras. I took this group to the wine cellar and a guy from a tour bus decided to go down with us. They were in there talking when all of a sudden the woman behind the bar gasped and said, "It went right through me!" and at the same time the guest that we invited took a picture, and when he went back and looked at his digital, you could see right through her. In the picture you could see the bottles right behind her. The cameras picked up the ghost going right through her.

The Santa Maria Inn.

One time we had a séance in the wine cellar, and I felt that people were joking around with the spirits, saying stuff like, "Is that an alien's head?" I felt their presence. I felt that when people began joking around, the spirits withdrew; that they felt that they weren't being taken seriously; that might explain how some of the orbs were leaving one by one; that was all captured by the cameras upstairs.

S [name protected] had an incident. She came into work early one morning and she was downstairs in her office. The housekeeping executive came in and they were sitting there, talking like this, and "I'm S and you're B [name protected], and we're having conversation," and all of sudden they both got quiet. Like froze, and B said "Did you see that?" I said, "What do you mean; I didn't see nothing," and she goes, "It went this way."

I miss the orbs. I really do. I'd go up there and sit there and watch (on the front desk camera), and then I'd run down (to the wine cellar) and see if I could see something.

One time we were out on the dance floor with the paranormal group and they were trying to get the spirits to talk, and they were saying stuff like, "We're gonna go out dancing now," you know, trying to get them to talk with their recorders, and you'll hear somebody say, "Have a nice dance," and it was a women's voice.

One time we were talking about the pictures up here, and because I heard the story before the hotel was built, that a child was killed. There's a picture of a guy standing with a child. Well, we were just talking, saying, "Do you think this is the child? And do you think that child's haunting the hotel?" And a voice comes back and says, "I don't." They picked up more words than they did on cameras.

A lot of stories; we've had employees say the TVs go off, when they open that door the TV just went off, or a hotel guest tells me they don't read magazines, but when they left the room and were only gone for two minutes, and came back to find all these magazines all over their bed. We had a guest years ago, way before my time, who called the front desk and said, "I hear music and there's people dancing." And he was told, "Well yeah, you hear music because you're over the bar." And he said, "Well no, there are people dancing in my room!" And we had another guest in 221 call down and say, "There's a woman hovering over me."

The Santa Maria Inn.

Next to room 221 is the painting of a woman, known as the "Mistress of the Sea Captain." The painting itself is very strange. The skin tone looks alive. A sallow blue gray; not "alive" but dead, in the sense that the painting does not look like a painting but a painting of a dead person, who really looks dead; corpse like. It has been said when the hotel staff tried to remove the painting strange things have happened. Her eyes seem to follow you as you walk down the hallway. An employee said that when he looked at the painting from an angle the face briefly morphed into a skull, and then returned to normal...

"They say this is the woman who was supposed to have been murdered," says a hotel employee who continues:

> For a while up in the hallway, and it was in front of 220, not 221, there was a dark spot, and it looked like where a body could have been lying. They shampooed it and it came right back, but now it's gone again, but for the longest time it was there. I would go upstairs and walk one way and you couldn't see it, walk the other way and you'd see it. I would go down and lie in it. It was here for the longest time because I'd show people, and then it was gone, and it hasn't been back since.

The Santa Maria Inn. Painting of the "Mistress of the Sea Captain."

Things have been seen in 219. A stain was next to the bed where they changed the carpet; people have seen it come back in the past, and they've seen it in 219 and 221. The stain reappeared after the carpet was changed. We've had our carpets changed since the happening, but if you look outside Room 220 you can see the stain of a body lying halfway out the door. Like the body of the mistress. It's always there, even though we lift up carpets and shampoo. The original site was built in 1917.

No one knows who murdered her, it could have been the captain, it could have been the captain's wife. And I've had guests tell me, we're walking down that hallway and they'll say, "You see that picture over there?" and I'll say, "Yes," and they'll say, "There something weird about that picture." I don't want to tell them anything because I don't want to scare our hotel guests, so I don't say nothing, just something like "Oh, maybe it's the way the light's shining on it."

When I stayed in the room and woke up the clock said "333"; other people told me that was the time the spirits come out; something woke me up, I don't know what.

There was one time, five years ago, when we were on a slow slump, and so we shut down the second floor in the tower just to save electricity. So nobody had been renting those rooms. This was during Christmas time, and then all of a sudden we started having some leaks coming down over by the gift shop. So they went running upstairs to the room above it which is the second floor; somebody had plugged up the bathtub and the water was overflowing, but that whole floor was closed; they never rented that room. They did an audit on the door and no one had entered that room with a key. Practical jokes like that, like you'll open the elevator door and you'll find furniture or fake plants or something like that, but nothing harmful.

"When I was 16 years old, I had a very close friend of mine die in a car accident," says an employee who explains:

...And after I went to his funeral, I came home... I could always feel that person touching my face saying "Don't cry, I'm okay," or if I'm lying in bed, I could feel that somebody is sitting in my bed, and you're looking around and there's nobody here. But somebody sat down on the bed and then I'll feel like a palm caressing my face. Like telling me, "Don't cry, no more tears," so when I finally was telling this to someone, they said just to tell him you'll be okay. They can go. You're okay. When you stop dwelling and quit thinking about that person's death and how much you missed them, they will go, and it did. When I said, "I'm gonna be okay now. I miss you, but I'm gonna be okay," it stopped, and about once in a great while I'll think of that person and I will feel that someone sit on my bed, even to this day and that's been....I'm 55 years old now. Every once in a while I'll feel that person sitting on my bed. He was 19 and I was 16. So from there I could believe there was life after death, and I know this guy had unfinished business. He died in a tragic accident.

Here, I think some of the ghosts are maybe people that stay here a lot, like one of the ghosts could be the owner. One of our owner's husbands had passed away five years ago before his dream of reopening the tap room. This hotel was his pride and he's still here, taking care of things.

Downstairs where the wine cellar is located is where all of our offices are, and I always felt like there's something down there. One day, I took one of the paranormal groups down there. First, I opened up my office and the temperature was scorching down there. I'm going, "It gets hot, but never this hot." Okay, so I open the door to the next office; it gets a little bit cooler, so I open the door to the catering office, and it was ice cold. They were all kinds of congregating in there, so as I stood by the door letting them do their thing, I felt a cold numbness go through my left side, and so I said, "What's here, what's beside me?" They said, "You have a small child standing there beside you." I said, "Okay, that's good." I took them to different places and we got to the staircase where we're supposed to go up and I said, "Is this person still with me?" And they said, "Yeah, she wants to play," so I just turned around and said, "You go back to my office and when we get done, I'll come downstairs and I'll play with you." So after that every time I see weird things happening in my office, or the temperature changes, I say, "You sit down right here, and when I get done with my work, we'll play." And then it stops. The lights will stop flickering or the temperature will change, and I'll say, "We'll play after I get done with my work." I have learned to talk to them.

Another employee went to the storage room by the basement. He put his key in the lock and unlocked it, then he said that suddenly the door just swung open, and I went downstairs and tried to push the door open. There is no wind down there, no windows, and it's too heavy to move by itself.

I've taken them all over the place, and the worst thing that really scared me was this room right here. This room used to be the original dining room of this hotel, so I took them in there and automatically they felt something, so they were going towards the south end of the room, and I stayed on the north end. I was *not* going to get near them. And then all of a sudden I felt somebody reaching into my pocket and was gonna grab something. I screamed. Nobody's around me because they're all on the south end of the room; nobody's around me, and I actually felt somebody get into my pocket, so they ran over here and they're going, "Yeah, there's somebody over here." And *ch ch ch*, they're taking pictures away, and they would talk. They picked up voices. We just remodeled that tap room seven years ago, so after we first reopened, it was closing time. At 2AM in the morning I turned all the lights up on the original side of the bar. I was sitting there talking to my bartenders, and all of a sudden, the lights all started differently turning on. Not at the same time, but different. I turned around and looked and I said, "Even you guys, get out of here, it's closing time!" It stopped. And this just happened a year ago. Another time we were standing behind the bar; it was a Friday, Saturday night. The lights went up, so I went running over there to see who was playing with the lights. Nobody was there, so I dimmed the lights back down, but then we looked back over. Our refrigeration, which is hard to open, all of a sudden started opening, and I told everybody, "Okay, if we see a beer floating out of there, that's it, bar's closed, we're all going home."

Okay, the bartender told us this story—I'm not sure how long ago it was, but we have an XM radio in our bar, and he said it was slow one night, so he turned on some 80s music and put it up full blast, and he walked away, and the music just stopped. So he said he went back there to check it, and the cord, which is not a cord that can easily be unplugged, was unplugged and swinging back and forth. So he said he plugged it back in, and then ten minutes later it happened again, so he went back and the cord was unplugged and swinging back and forth even *faster.* And he said, "Okay." He plugged it back in, and he never turned it back up that loud again, and it never happened again.

I've been in the tap room, and I'm seeing out of the side, and I've seen an older man and he stands there. And I turned around and I'm like okay, its all good. And I've found out that if you talk to them, it's okay...but if you're ignoring them, and they want your attention [raps on the table], they're gonna get your attention.

There's times you go to the elevator and you don't have to even punch the button; the elevator door will open, and I've gotten to the point where I'll say, "Thank you! Would you like to *join* me? Or ride up to the room with me?" We've had cooks in the past that will say...we've had this piano [the one in the historical room] and it was playing on its own. And it wasn't a player piano, it was a regular piano, and we actually called the police to have them check it out.

We have one person in the kitchen. He's no longer with us, but he would tell me stories that when he's here by himself, cleaning up the kitchen after everybody's gone, and he'll find pans flying down, things will fall and he'll pick them up and put them back. And they're playing games with him again and he finally he tells them: "I DON'T HAVE TIME FOR YOUR GAMES RIGHT NOW. PUT IT BACK," and they'll stop.

The manager could actually see people coming out of the walls; his desk would be the only thing behind him, and there would be a wall, and he would actually feel somebody like this (puts hand on her shoulder), and he would tell them, "I don't have time for this now," and they would go away. Nobody could have come up behind him without him noticing it.

Another employee was in the kitchen getting coffee, and the metal tins that we put food on started spinning, and then just stopped. He ran out of the kitchen. They're starting to play now. Maybe a year will go by and nobody's encountering anything, but lately people are encountering so that means they're starting to play again.

CHAPTER THREE

THE PARANORMAL ACTIVITY OF VENTURA COUNTY

THE BELLE MAGGIORE INN

SYLVIA LIVES ON

Guests at the charming and lovely Belle Maggiore Inn in Ventura enjoy their stay so much they don't want to check out. One such guest is Sylvia Michaels, one of the few resident spirits at Belle Maggiore Inn.

Profile: Age twenty-three at time of death.

Persona: A sad spirit who was said to have fallen in love with a sailor while working as a prostitute during Belle Maggiore's "flop house days." Loves to dance on the stairs, and possesses an energy described as "cold." Enjoys getting into bed with men, and the occasional woman. Can sometimes be heard crying over her lost love. Her "claim to fame" is appearing on "Haunted Hotels," and a three part series on the Travel Channel that aired in 2001. She stays in room number 17.

Her signature scent is...

"The first day I came to work, there was the stench of rose perfume, like that old rose perfume from the 40s, like your grandma would have? Just in my face. I smell it often," says a front desk clerk.

It's the same thing every time, and it's very déjà vu familiar. One night I was sitting here and it was a very quiet Sunday night. Even the guests noticed it was very quiet. I was just sitting here, and then I heard, "Hey I'm up here." Like twice, like UP, a little voice, soft spoken. It was like if someone were whispering to you. Faint, but it felt like it was up and in the room. Then it was like a week ago I was up there, and I was walking down the hall and I thought I heard someone say my name, but it was friendly. It was a, "Hey." Later that night I was walking to put stuff away in the back room, and as I was coming back, for some reason, and I don't know if it's because I was passing by that area, but I looked down and my scarf was gone. I felt it come off me, and I looked behind and my scarf was on the floor. I had a sweater on, and this is a scarf that won't slip off with that sweater, and I didn't feel it come off me whatsoever and usually you can tell. It was almost as if like...oh I get chills, and it was right when I passed Sylvia's room.

Room 24 on Halloween night. A woman staying in the room looked in the mirror and took a photo. I could make out three different faces. You can see the folds in her braids. In the corner by the TV you can see a little kid's face and another face close to it, and if you look at in a different light, I'm not kidding, it almost looks like there's a party going on....there's this wispy whatever.

A manager at the inn relates her own experience.

I have two computers in my office, one that faces room 17, and one that faces what is known as the Courtyard Café. My office is located right next to room 17. I'm in room 16 as an office, and on the TV we only watch channel 63. *Fox News*, that's all we watch. We never change channels on this computer. It's an old DOS computer. You have to double click on the TV icon, and it takes about a minute for it to even come on. I came into my office, put my purse down, went to my computer, was checking my e-mails, and all of a sudden the DOS computer came on, and it was the *Montel* show with Sylvia Brown. She's a psychic, and the ghost next door is named Sylvia. My back was to that computer. I heard Montel and I turned around and I looked, and I was like "whoa" and then I listened. , It was Sylvia Brown on the *Montel* show. I listened to what was being said in case there was a message I needed to hear. But I was so overwhelmed and I didn't know if I should move, and my telephone is right by that computer that turned on, and so I just kind of sat there a little bit and listened. And then I looked around. I was more nervous than anything. This was about two and a half years ago. It was during the day and I was alone. It was around ten o'clock in the morning. I let the program finish, and then I changed it back to *Fox News* and it stayed there. I just kind of blew that incident off, and I didn't really tell anyone about it, and then two weeks after that, the shutters in my office and the windows...I walked into my office, the lights were on, the TV was on, and when I walked into my office I could smell roses, and it was SO thick, that I could walk through it. I just gently put my purse down and backed out of the office and closed the door. Sylvia smells like roses. She was a prostitute, and some say that she either hung herself or she was murdered, but what I really honestly think is that she was murdered, and that she has been waiting for a relative or the person that murdered her to come back and apologize, and that's the only reason she sticks around.

The Belle Maggiore Inn lobby.

She doesn't like men, and she used to play tricks. She would hide their wallet, which would make sense because she used to be a prostitute. We had some guests—they went out to dinner and came back. The husband couldn't find his wallet; they were looking everywhere; she puts it in weird spots, you know that mesh part in your backpack where you don't really put stuff? It was in there, and the backpack was in the closet.

This hotel used to be a brothel. I was sitting in Nana's Courtyard Café with a very good friend who is a psychic, and she was facing the building and I was facing the street, and she looks at me and says, "Who's the woman in the champagne dress who keeps walking back and forth across the balcony with her hair in a bun?"

The Belle Maggiore Inn.

And she said Sylvia was lost and didn't want to leave, because she didn't hang herself. She was murdered, and she didn't want to leave until she got an apology, and it didn't even have to be an apology from the person, but from a relative that would be staying here and then wake up and apologize. The majority of psychics here say that she was murdered, and because she was a prostitute, they just let it go.

Then we have this little girl who was thrown off the balcony by her stepfather. The stepfather threw her off the balcony, and she was abused, and she's still here. M M came to do a video. In the video her hair was just twisting by itself, and then it just dropped. They think it was the little girl playing with her hair. In one room they found a child's handprint and the phone was off the hook.

She walks the halls
Up the stairs
With the delicate wrought iron leaf grillwork
And hovers around Room 17.

From the poem "Sylvia," written in 1993

Sylvia is not the only ghost engaged in paranormal activity at the Belle Maggiore, as an employee explains.

We were staying in room 36 in July or August 2009. There were around three of us in the room with some children. The little boy woke up every night around two or three, and was just screaming bloody murder, and it took my sister about an hour or hour and a half to get him back to bed. He didn't like being left alone. We didn't figure out what was going on until a couple of months later we heard about a ghost who would show himself to children. He's pushed a man out the balcony, I think room 31, but I know that his daughter used to play on the balcony and he supposedly pushed her off the balcony as well.

The Belle Maggiore Inn.

The Belle Maggiore Inn.

When the author stayed at the inn she related the following experience:

> I woke up around 1:30-2AM and I heard these two people arguing outside. That's when the swirling white mist appeared and seemed to get into my bed. I knew it was a ghost. It was interesting because it was really noisy outside. I was in room 3. I heard a couple outside start to argue—a woman: "F------ a------, what are you doing to me?" And the man was also angry. And it was right at that point when the ghost appeared to me. The next day when I spoke to the manager, she intuitively said, "I think it was the little girl" (a resident ghost). A little girl was tagging around with me and wouldn't leave my side. She said she could see her clinging to my left leg. When I asked her what side she was on, she said the left side. My lower left side had been tingling. In the hotel room she had been sitting Indian style next to me. I went out and bought a stuffed bear angel at the angel shop and left it in her room. I promised I would send her some post cards so that the manager could read them to her. I think that the little girl manifested herself because she was scared. She wanted to get into bed with me because she was scared of the voices outside. The manager gave me a bracelet so that I could keep the energy of the girl.

THE CANDLELIGHT KITCHEN AND BAR AND THE "MADAME BUTTERFLY" OF VENTURA

In Puccini's tragic opera *Madame Butterfly,* Cho Cho san is left behind by B. F. Pinkerton, a Lieutenant in the United States Navy. She waits three long years for his return, having his child in the interim. "Oh, Butterfly, my little wife, I shall return with the roses, when the earth is full of joy, when the robin makes his nest." Suzuki quietly begins to weep. Butterfly says that, "one beautiful day" they will see a puff of smoke on the far horizon. Then a ship will appear and enter the harbor.[28]

Legend has it that the Carlo Hahn House was home to Rosa, a young daughter of an Italian immigrant family in the 1800s. Forced into a loveless marriage, she found love in the arms of a young Italian sailor, who, much like Pinkerton, left her pregnant as he left for the sea...Rosa was said to have committed suicide, and left to roam the Italianate mansion forever, walking on the staircase, or staring out of the window on the second floor searching for her ship to returns to its harbor, just as Cho Cho san had searched Nagasaki Harbor for Pinkerton's ship...

"Quella destinata per te, nessuno la prenderà."

Translation: "True love waits."

Such was not the case for Cho Cho san or Rosa...

The co-owner related his own experience.

> KBBY did a show here. They were doing haunted houses, and they came in with equipment, and they were taking pictures. They saw some orbs and stuff, and through the years we've had organizations with all their meters. One time they asked if they could come, and they said it would be after hours, so they were here for a few hours with all kinds of meters and they were doing all kinds of stuff. I can't verify anything. I just said, "That's kind of interesting." Me, I'm more of a realist.
>
> I've owned this for ten years. Landmark 78, that was the previous name. Now it's called the "Candlelight Kitchen and Bar." The plaque outside notes that it's Historical Landmark 78. It gets that status from the historical society of this area. In the 1970s it was a house, and then converted into a restaurant. Now I'm the co-owner.
>
> In 1912, Carol Hann had this house built for him and his wife, and I guess he was also a sailor. He went off on a journey, and went out to sea, I guess she was feeling lonely and had sexual relations with another guy. She was so distraught she ended up hanging herself, and that's now the ladies' room. I guess it used to be a bedroom. She had an Italian lover. She hung herself before he could come back. She was so ashamed of what she did.
>
> My wife has had experiences. She was sitting down with our newborn and the lights just came on, and we said, "Oh, I guess Rosa decided she needed lights." [Rosa is the name of the woman.] And

then they were off, and I asked "Are you sure they were on?" We've had people come in for dinner and they've asked, "Who's the lady in the red dress in the bathroom?" And they didn't know the story, and the story was that she had been walking down the stairs in a red dress. For me personally, I didn't see it, but I'm a realist.

The Candlelight Kitchen and Bar.

I've heard the voices on their tapes. Just a lot of whispering, that's all I could make out. Believe it or not, we've had alarm systems, brand new, and they didn't work, and they came and replaced them, and they didn't work again. And it was like, what's going on with this building, something about Rosa and electronics. We've had monitors burn out prematurely and gotten them replaced. It's kind of weird that two brand new alarm systems burn out, basically the brain boxes. Even the alarm system guy said, "I've never seen anything like that. I've seen one burnt out but never two."

Another employee at the restaurant had this to say.

> I was here late. Everybody else had left, and you know how you feel when you're not alone. That was it, just a feeling. It was creepy. I had never felt that. I've worked in a 20,000-foot-square building by myself at four o'clock in the morning and never felt that.

THE FRESH MEX RESTAURANT

Located in Oxnard, the Fresh Mex Restaurant has been around for about forty years. The only items on the menu that even resemble the paranormal are the California Cosmo and the Hypno-Rita. The restaurant, however, has its own juicy tidbits that have been devoured over the years.

"This building has been around since I've been a kid," says an employee at the restaurant and continues:

> It's over forty years old. From what I've heard it's not really an aggressive entity, but just lets people know it's here. Actually, something just happened to me last week on Thursday. I was lying down on a booth in the VIP room, and as I'm lying down, I put my foot on the table and I pick up my phone. I start to doze off, and all of sudden I get really tired. And I'm dozing and I thought it was one of the employees or my brother, and I felt like something was standing over the table glaring at me, and I opened my eyes and there's nothing there. I started to doze off and I see that silhouette again. I had my phone and it's sitting at the edge of the table, and as I started to get off, I'm sure I saw something and then it's gone.
>
> There's times when we have the door closed and I'm at the bar and there are these little windows, and you can see someone just walking by going towards the exit and you see no door open. Nothing. With the bar lights, it's always one light that stays on. We turn it off at night and it just turns back on, and the funny thing is that it's called a "hypnotic," and it's funny that that's the light that flickers on and off, and it's a brand new light. All this equipment is brand new. When we leave at night we turn off all the lights, and

it's the same crew that opens up in the morning and closes, and we know that we turned the light off, and in the morning it's totally on and functioning properly. There are times when we're turning it off and it won't turn off, and I'm just like I'm gonna leave it on, and in the morning it's off! And I know I left it on. We have sensors on all the doors, so whenever we open the doors, we hear beeping sounds in the main hall.

Sometimes we'll be the only two in here and we'll hear the alarm go off...sometimes you walk in here and it's *freezing cold*, and there's a very *strong* odor that overtakes this room and sometimes the whole restaurant. Like a sewer smell, and we've had plumbers in here and we had the city come in here, and they can't find anything wrong in here. Like disgustingly overwhelming, and it's not the plumbing and they can't figure out what it is. We've replaced the piping into the street, and we've brought professional plumbers out here. They have no solution for it. It still comes back. The smell—it happens sporadically and randomly. I've heard so many things about this place. I heard there used to be a studio above us, and there was a fire and the lady perished. I've heard that this was her business and that she put all her money into it and she still wants to see it successful. I heard that only women get harassed. Nudged, pushed, hair tugged, because it's another woman. The women argue, "This is my place." But the sewage smell is really, really bad. Our maintenance guy here tries to do little tricks to cover up the smell, like put little table covers down at the edges of the door, spray everything, close the curtains, open up the doors, sometimes it's a weird, weird smell.

The odd thing was when we first opened, we had a lady come in and I've never seen her again. She came in, she was telling me the history and saying, "It's a female." She knew everything. She said, "I used to sit right here." And she's never come back ever again. I find that odd for someone who was a regular back then, who knew the history of this place, to tell me all this stuff and never come back again. She was saying, "When I was here twenty years ago, this is what happened."

Little fruit fly bugs? They come everywhere. We found them flying around our plants the other day. We cleaned really, really well so there's no reason for them to be here, but they seem to always keep coming back. We'll see them flying everywhere. I don't know what they're attracted to, but they are constantly a nuisance, and it's a new building. Everything was redone, but it's like these little flies are everywhere, even if there's no food around.

The first rumor that I heard that someone died here was the lady who lived in the studio above, but it could be just a rumor. When we opened we had a bishop bless the place. Came in and did the holy water; did the reading of the Bible and he even left us some water; he didn't find anything evil in this place. I'm pretty sure the spirit that's in here took it as a positive thing.

I have a daughter; she's two and half years old. We'd always come in here and have lunch, and I'd set her in the VIP room and she'd sit there and eat her food. I'd run off and do something real quick, and I could hear giggling and laughing and talking, and I'd come back and I thought she was playing with her toy from McDonald's, "Happy Man;" but she was just doing it on her own. I know that kids have that extra sense. I never thought anything of it until we opened and people would start saying, "Yeah this place is haunted." Some of our servers always feel there is somebody right behind them. They see like shadows and dark spots.

Fresh Mex Restaurant.

Another employee says,

> Some guys were doing some work here and standing next to the bar and one of the guys got pushed. Something just pushed him. His brother told me one day he had seen like a shadow, walking through this area right here, and we were the only two here. The smell—it goes by section. First starts here, then there, and if we don't stop it, it will consume the whole restaurant.

VENTURA CITY HALL

WITH OUR GUIDE, RICHARD SENATE

We were the lima bean capital of the nation. There is a lima bean carving on the front of the courthouse. We were a ranching community. The natives were trained to be *vaqueros*. All the Latino families lost their land to the Americans, sometimes for seven cents an acre. They were looking for a new crop to grow. There was a new crop from South America called "lima beans." We mispronounced the name. It was a dry crop. You didn't have to water it, but they had a problem. The Americans didn't mind making the money but actually planting the beans?? No, no, no. Harvesting them? They asked the Latinos to do it. They laughed because they were *vaqueros,* cowboys, and didn't want to do it, so they brought in the Chinese laborers to do this. We had a lima bean queen, we had lima bean festivals. In 1897, at the World's Fair, Ventura's contribution to the California pavilion was a [illegible]7 foot pagoda made out of lima beans. Lima beans paid for the taxes on this building. We went directly from there to oil. We became an oil town. The first offshore oil drilling was done right off our coast. We had oil fields rivaling the best of Texas.

Every major trial was held here in this courthouse. In 1963, we had an earthquake. This building was deemed unsafe, so the county was going to tear it down, but the city bought it for $140,000 and sank $4M into it to make it earthquake safe. Now we've used it in a lot of movies—*The Two Jakes*, the sequel to *Chinatown*. A number of other movies, TV shows. Disney comes up here a lot. They come here and tape, and we get the money.

Ventura City Hall.

THE FLOATING HEAD

Right after this place was opened, we began to hear stories of ghosts. We have several accounts. One is a bizarre story of a floating head. Just a head, no body. The head seems to move like it has a body. I think it has a body, but it's invisible to us. There is something in the materialization process that wasn't complete. A man did see a head and also a shadow. I did some research. Two judges died in this building. One of a heart attack and the other suicide. The suicide was sad because it was a really popular young judge. Everyone thought he had a great career, but he got caught up in a scandal. This wealthy family had a bad son who got thrown out of college. One night he was at a party, late, and drove home drunk, and there was a poor kid delivering newspapers. He killed him. He didn't stop, but there was a witness who saw it, a farmer, and he identified the kid and his fancy car, and he was caught. The case was thrown out of court because there wasn't enough evidence, and they found out the family had given the judge like $10,000 in cash, so when that came out, the judge went into his office and shot himself.

MA DUNCAN...NOT A NICE LADY

A ghost was linked to the biggest case ever tried here in 1959. A lady named Elizabeth (Ma) Duncan hired two men to kill her pregnant daughter-in-law because she hated her, and they did it. She lived in Santa Barbara. Her daughter-in-law was Olga Duncan. Big famous case. She paid the men $6,000 to murder her. They implicated the mother. At the time, it was like the O.J. Simpson trial; reporters from all over the nation. It went on for three months, and every day new revelations. All kinds of sexy stuff—the lady ran a brothel and slept with her own son. She did all kinds of bizarre things. Had been married twenty-two times. A bigamist, and she was sentenced to death, which by the way is really weird because in Ventura County we don't sentence women to death. Some say it's because she was from Santa Barbara. While she was on death row about to be executed, she managed to unscrew a light bulb in her cell, break the glass up, put it in orange juice, and tried to get the guards to drink it, which would have killed them; so she's trying to murder someone while she is waiting for an execution. Not a nice lady, so if anybody would come back and be ghoulish, it would be her. In the courtroom a lot of people have gotten orbs. Ma Duncan has been seen in a gray prison dress in the corner.

Ventura City Hall.

Ventura City Hall. Statue of Father Junipero Serra.

There's a real fancy alarm system...we know the system works because late at night somebody pushes the panic button, and the lights go on and the police come, but there's nobody there. Some people have told me that it's cold in this room when that happens. That's another consistent thing. A strange coldness linked to ghosts. It's first mentioned in the "Epic of Gilgamesh." The freezing cold was mentioned. To manifest themselves they draw energy from the living, and we detect that loss as a chill or cold. It's not a real cold, it's a psychic cold, and if you've ever felt it, you won't mistake the two, it's quite different. Real cold is like on the surface going down, from the outside of your skin going in. Psychic cold is from the inside going out. It gets right to your bones. Many times you'll feel the cold or the chill just before something happens, so if you feel a chill, be on your mark, because something might be about to happen.

THE WOMAN IN A RED DRESS

There is the story of the woman in the red dress in city hall—they saw her, but they never saw her face. They saw her from behind.

They could tell she had a red hat. Who wears a hat today, right? A red jacket, padded shoulders, a short skirt, pencil skirt, and seams up the back of her stockings. The style looks like something from 1943 or 1945. She was headed right for the door, and they saw her reach out for the door handle, and then she disappeared. All the people saw her, so my wife was screaming, I'm downstairs. I of course come up, there's nothing here except some very panic stricken people.

One guy said, "I could die now that I've seen a ghost," but I think this is an angry woman about to confront her husband about having a mistress on the side. The story was that she later took her own life, shot herself, or did herself in one of a number of ways. But she has been detected since, I believe the early story is 1948 and they have gotten up to 1995; so a period of years will pass, but then they'll get the footsteps, high-heeled shoes, or see this apparition.

I had a group here and one of the ladies was very dramatic. She said, "I'm feeling something," and so just to play along I said, "If you're here, make yourself known." Very dramatic. Now what did I expect to happen? Nothing, but the dang lights go on in that office! And I thought, *Maybe there's somebody here, and they turned the lights on.* So I went in there and there's nobody there. I checked the whole place, in the back rooms and stuff, hoping to find someone who could have turned the light on. There was nobody here to do that.

Question from the author: You said you heard the high heels of a woman in the courthouse but the hallway was carpeted. How would you explain that?

Because the sounds we were getting were probably created back in 1940 when they had a tiled floor. A retrocognitive sound from World War II. In essence, the sound was created on the tile which no longer existed here. The high-heeled woman—some say she shot herself, others say she threw herself off the pier. It could be that she was walking down the hall and that confrontation was being reenacted to confront her husband who was cheating on her. All talk about an air of anger and hate.

The elevator that goes up to the third floor is not just used for storage; it was the old women's jail. You can see the ghosts there as well. It's kind of like a big attic now. In the women's jail—in 1941 before the Ma Duncan trial, a lady hung herself in her cell and we don't know why, because she was just picked up for writing bad checks, and it wasn't a serious crime, but she hung herself and that cell was considered haunted. They didn't like to use it because people incarcerated there had nightmares. We held a séance there to try and find out why she hung herself, and she said that she had murdered a man. Nobody knew about it but she thought it would come out, and the guilt was so great she took her own life, but séances are notoriously unpredictable, and we can't say that what comes out of them as being gospel.

Escape Gone Wrong

There is a story back in the 1950s of a man who tried to escape the jail. At that time, the men's exercise yard was being renovated, so they let the men prisoners exercise on the roof, and he managed to get a sheet and rip it into rope and tie it around his waist. He had two of his friends do a demonstration, and he went over the wire. He got over the wire and he tried to go down the rope he made. Unfortunately, it ripped and he plunged to this death. Know the sad thing? Nobody knew he was missing, not until a guy went out to lunch and tripped over his body, so now his ghost is seen.

Hallway in Ventura City Hall.

Again it might be that he was thinking—should I go down or should I not? And he did it anyway and fell to his death, and maybe that intense moment is why he is seen—reenacting his last attempt to escape. His ghost has been seen running on this ledge, mostly in the corner. When I worked for the city I proposed doing a ghost tour. Some of the people got an orb right in that very corner. According to traditions, that's where he fell to his death.

The Chumash believed there are three worlds—the upper world, middle world, and underworld. The middle world was where people lived, the underworld for demons, and the sky creatures were the upper world. There was the rattlesnake god, the turtle god, and various spirits of demons. We had a Chumash Shaman come and perform a ritual that invoked the spirit of Heleke, the hawk.

The Earl Stanley Gardener building on the corner of California and Main Street is haunted. It is where the lawyer Earl Stanley Gardener had his office on the third floor and wrote Perry Mason in 1930. On Main Street Ventura there was a Spanish restaurant where all of the waitresses were dressed in flamenco outfits—dresses, combs in their hair, high-heeled shoes. They still see them, as ghosts, walking around back there in these fancy red dresses. The old Spanish Mission, San Buenaventura, on Main Street is haunted by two ghosts—a lady in white and a phantom padre in a gray robe.

Ventura City Hall – ledge of the running.

There used to be a large tree that was used by the locals as a hanging tree. It was on the Corner of Ventura Avenue and Main Street. These tall eucalyptus trees on Harbor Boulevard are important because every February the monarch butterflies land here for the migratory thrust coming up from Mexico. A couple of days a year these are so full of butterflies you can't see the green leaves anymore. There are millions of them. The Mexicans believe that the butterfly is the spirit of a dead person.

OLIVAS ADOBE

CASA DE PHANTASAMAS

El Museo Olivas Adobe es refugio de almas en pena. Construido en 1847 y llamado Rancho Santa Fe, fue edificado por don Raymundo, un rico y generoso hacendado muy querido por la comunidad, quien vivió allí hasta 1899 con su esposa Teodora y sus 21 hijos….

...which means...

The Museum Olives Adobe is a refuge of souls in pain. Constructed in 1847 and called Farm Santa Fe, it was built by Raymundo Olivas, a rich and generous landowner very loved by the community; he lived there until 1899 with his wife Teodora and their 21 children.[29]

The Olivas Adobe, registered as California Historical Landmark #115, is an adobe built in 1841 by Raymundo Olivas, a Mexican citizen who came to Los Angeles and made his fortune in cattle ranching. Blessed with wealth, children, and beloved by the community, what is it about the Olivas Adobe that would earn the title of "a refuge of souls in pain?"

The adobe is said to be one of the most haunted houses in the western United States, with paranormal activity being experienced on a regular basis. Lights have turned on by themselves around 2AM in the morning and stayed on all night. Dolls have been moved in the children's room. Music boxes play by themselves. A lady in a black nineteenth-century dress gazes out the second floor window, while a ghost face has been seen at a window of the children's room. EVPs have been recorded of children giggling and a woman humming at the balcony. Perhaps it was the very wealth of the Olivas family that made them the target of robberies, starting in 1855 when bandits attacked the family for their gold. In *The Ghosts and Legends of the Olivas Adobe,* it is quoted that, "The bandits came and ransacked the house pausing only to strike Mrs. Olivas with their pistols and rip the gold pierced earrings from her ears. She screamed so loud she was unable to speak for a month."[30]

Another tragedy occurred at the Olivas Adobe, that could explain the presence of another apparition that has been seen of a young woman in a white slip with bloody sockets for eyes. Psychics determined the girl was raped and blinded by a male Yankee guest staying at the home. He strangled her and then escaped. The men of the Olivas family hunted him down and dragged him back to the adobe where they took a knife to him and dumped his body in the Santa Clara River.[31]

Olivas Adobe.

In 1911, a silent western called *Mission Waif* was shot in Ventura by French movie maker Gaston Melies. Two years later, Gaston Melies shot another silent film at Ventura's historic Olivas Adobe called *The Gringo Strikes*.[32]

If a present-day ghost story were to be filmed at Olivas Adobe, it would certainly boast an impressive cast of characters—The Ghostly Girl in White, The Phantom Cook, The Eyeless Lady, and The Owls of the Olivas Adobe. Native American superstition believes that owls only built their nests near haunted places. Some American Indian tribes associate owls with death, and that owls may accompany the soul of the deceased as it makes it way to the next world. Since the 1940s, the Olivas Adobe has been the home of a family of owls who build their nest in one of the large trees that shade the courtyard. The owls are great horned owls, the largest of the owl family. Like the owls, the legends and spirits of the Olivas Adobe continue to entertain the people of the Central Coast.[33]

Nationwide ghost hunter Richard Senate has experienced various paranormal events at the Olivas Adobe.

> I saw this dang ghost of a little girl. She was seen over and over again. A guy came with a camera to take a picture of her, so he was there and we were upstairs. He would call out her name and she would appear, pretty consistent too. Finally, he called her name out and he was taking a picture. All of his batteries went dead. She was just a fuzzy form. She was taking the energy from the batteries of the camera and using it. A lady had a cell phone and that battery went dead, and this is consistent over and over again, especially in poltergeist cases. We were investigating a poltergeist case and every time we tried to get a picture? The batteries would go dead. My advice was to get an old camera, the kind that uses gears, like a WW2 wind up 16 mm camera, then get special "candlelight" film, load it up with that; they tried it and they actually got the apparitions on camera. Ghosts can manipulate electronics.

THE GLEN TAVERN INN

OF GHOSTS AND GAMBLERS

It is a spring night in the Glen Tavern Inn in Santa Paula, circa 1900. Gaston Melies, silent film director of *The Ghost of Sulphur Mountain* and world sailor, is engaged in a game of poker with another infamous guest, Calvin, who likes his clothing western, his hair long, and his cigars expensive. A blonde prostitute named Jessie looks on, smiling at Calvin as he returns from the washroom, where he had indecently loaded a stack of cards, fours and kings, into his dinner napkin. Melies's eyes are on Jessie.

In twelve years, the *Titanic* would sink, but at this point, no one cares.

Calvin returns to the table and passes the deck to Melies to cut, and then turns away to open up a new bottle of whiskey, then offers a glass of whiskey to Jessie, who is lounging against the wall.

She takes the glass, smiling at Calvin with prostitute eyes.

"One night, somebody caught Calvin cheating."

As the hand is picked up, we see that Melies has four eights, Calvin four fours, the rest of the players nothing. Calvin throws a chip on the table "Raise $100."

Melies throws five chips onto the table. "Raise $500."

Calvin sips his whiskey and sits the glass on the table, before raising $2,000.

Jessie's eyes widen.

Melies speaks slowly. "Your $2,000. I'll re-raise you $5,000."

Calvin leans back in his chair and takes another sip of whiskey. "I'm all in."

Jessie sits down. "I think I need another glass of whiskey."

Calvin pours her another glass and sets it down in front of her. "Here you are lovely lady." He looks at Melies.

Melies puts down his four eights. Calvin stares at them for a moment, and then lays down his cards. He looks up. "Four kings."

"They shot Calvin in the head, put a rope around his body."

Melies stares at them, his face growing pale. He turns over the entire deck and sees a king. He looks up. "You cheating bastard."

Jessie stares at him. "Honey, you look like that ghost in that movie of yours."

"...and lowered him to the basement through the dumbwaiter."

She stands up. "It's getting too hot for me. I need some air."

Calvin stands up. "I think I'll join you darlin'. It looks like my card playing finesse is not appreciated here."

Melies stands up and pulls out a pistol. "Sit down. Both of you. Have another drink before you go."

"A blonde prostitute had her head removed, and then her corpse deposited via a dumbwaiter that was used to smuggle liquor upstairs during Prohibition." [34]

Meet the ghosts of Glen Tavern Inn. An employee at the hotel relates his experience.

The Glen Tavern Inn Ghost Photo. Courtesy of The Glen Tavern Inn.

In the 1920s there was a brothel. There was a poker game going on, and in the poker game there was this one guy winning all night long. The other gentlemen, I'm sure after rounds and rounds of booze, had a shotgun and killed the other player. The loser killed the winner. Aside from that, this room was supposedly where the prostitute was beheaded.

From my knowledge, this is the closet that the body had been stored in. Also down the hall there's this little door that's now filled with electrical wires. That used to be part of the chute where alcohol used to come from the first floor all the way up to the third floor during prohibition, and there were rumors that the girl's body had been stuffed up in that or in this closet.

One really weird story—I had some friends stay here a few years ago. They were in this room, and they woke up in the morning to the alarm going off in the room across the hall, which is 306, and the alarm was going off for about an hour, so they finally went downstairs and said to the guy, "Hey is there anyone else staying down on the third floor? There's an alarm that went off across the hall." He looked through the books. No record of anybody, so they get up to the third floor and they get out the master key. They get to the doorway. The alarm had stopped. They put the key in, light turns green, didn't open. It was dead bolted from the inside, which was physically impossible. The only way to unlock a door is to get a ladder and go through the window. There's no way you can close the door behind you and have the dead bolt latch. It's impossible.

There was a polio epidemic going on at one point, and we housed a small hospital in 218 and on the second floor. A lot of children died.

It's always been a hotel but there have been different aspects to it. In room 218 there was a guy who took care of a lot of the children. A lot of them did die of polio. I'm not sure if this was during the war. There is a man who is a businessman. He's down the hall from 218. He's heard children laughing, he's heard footsteps. I've heard footsteps. I was walking down to my room. I had my key out. It's the only room that takes a key and not a key card, and I stopped to put the key in. The next thing you know I can still hear (makes the sound of sandals) and I turned around real quick and the noise stopped. I could still hear what sounded like my sandals. I could still hear footsteps coming down the hall behind me.

P [name protected] is an employee here, and it was I'd say two weeks ago, she rented out the penthouse, the Harry Houdini room. He has stayed there in the past. So she stayed there, not expecting anything. Her and her boyfriend stayed there. It was a birthday surprise for him. She filled the room with balloons. Throughout the night everything was fine. They said they only got about twenty minutes of sleep. Everything was just so spooky. They could hear the door knob rattling, footsteps walking through the room, noises coming from the bathroom. And the balloon—it looked like someone had pulled down the balloon halfway, and then it moved-from the kitchen to the living room, and that's when she got up and popped every balloon. She actually saw the balloon dropping down halfway, and then it was pulled ten feet away from all the other balloons. And that was when she almost left and went home. She doesn't live too far. Harry Houdini—the train broke down and he needed a place to stay; he needed the biggest room in the house because he had to sleep with all his props, and so he carried them all up to the third floor.

The Glen Tavern Inn Ghost Photo. Courtesy of The Glen Tavern Inn.

SLEEP PARALYSIS AT THE GLEN TAVERN INN

It's 2AM. You wake up with the feeling of something sitting on your chest. You can't move. You can't talk. You are half awake, half asleep, and fully paralyzed. Are you the victim of sleep paralysis, a seizure, or a witch sitting on your chest? "Sleep paralysis" or "SP," has been defined within both the medical and paranormal realm. A typical paranormal episode would include the victim not being able to move, great anxiety or fear, and a feeling of pressure on the chest, which may be related to the Incubus phenomenon—where a ghost tries to have sex with a victim. The film *The Entity* is one of the most famous documented cases of this phenomenon, based on a true story of a California woman who claimed to have experienced repeated sexual attacks from a spirit. Victims of the "Old Hag" syndrome wake up to find themselves paralyzed by a great weight on their chest, and the feeling of an evil presence in the room. SP has been defined in medical terms as relating to possible seizure disorders occurring during sleep. A few employees have experienced sleep disorders at the Glen Tavern Inn.

"It's a very scary feeling and you become quite panicked," says a woman well acquainted with the hotel. She continues to say:

> Either they want to be one with you, or they want to scare you to leave the place. I had that experience once. I'm more afraid of the living than the dead. The living can do horrendous things to you, but with the dead it's like energy that got stuck, and it's here, in a building that's almost 100 years old, you can imagine all the experiences, the weddings, people always want to connect to the past. There is something about nostalgia that's very magical, or people want to stay in that moment. They want to remember a time or they don't want to leave. I can think of a couple experiences from my childhood I'd like to go back to, and I know that this place had a lot of magical moments. The weddings here—high energy like you wouldn't believe.

Another employee at the hotel shared his experience.

That's happened to me, three times total, each time in different rooms in the hotel. I was like half asleep, half awake. It really freaked me out because I couldn't move, I couldn't talk. I started breathing really heavily. I was really freaked out because I hadn't been able to move for like the past seven-ten minutes.

The first two times it happened, I kind of like brushed it off. The second time I just disregarded it and fell asleep. The third time it like really hit me; it was just really, really strange because there's like this crazy anxiety running through your body, and you're paralyzed and you can't move. There's this crazy fear running through your body, and you either snap out of it, or some people will just fall asleep and just brush it off. I've only experienced it at the inn. It happened three times over the course of eighteen months. The third time I felt like there was someone there. My girlfriend was in bed with me, but it felt like somebody else was there. The first few times it didn't feel like anyone was there, but there was this overwhelming rush of fear and again you're paralyzed. You're mentally awake. You're conscious, but you're not moving. You have the most terrible fear you can ever experience. Sometimes you hallucinate. Who knows, but I've only had it happen to me here, and other guests have reported it as well.

I've had other experiences as well—three-four experiences total—the tail of 2007, once in 2008, and once, maybe two or three months ago. The first two happened within two-three days of each other. It was, I want to say October of 2007, both happened in the evening. I was sitting in the lobby by myself, waiting for a band member to come down, and then the keyboard started clicking, and a tin of pencils fell over as soon as I walked over. It was nine o'clock in the evening. The computer keyboard behind the desk. The keys started moving. Individually. It was like "*click. click*." So I walked over to the desk; no one was over there, and as I approached the desk. A tin of pencils fell over, and that was my first visit to the inn. Within that same first visit I experienced, after researching it, what was called "sleep paralysis." One of my band mates had an experience. There is a woman in white who only appears to males, down one of the hallways. We were all in the lobby, and he came up to us and said, "There's a woman walking around in a nightgown." Over the years, we've amassed a few resident spirits.

The Glen Tavern Inn.

THE PIERPONT INN

GLAMOUR AND GHOSTS

Sunday is Karaoke night at the Pierpont Inn in Ventura. You can boom out tunes from the psychedelic seventies, the nostalgic nineties, and of course the ecstatic eighties...neon letters flash out from a black screen: "Putting on the Ritz." Climb into a Pierce Arrow and race down memory lane to the Roaring Twenties, when the Pierpont Inn was in swinging form. Experience balmy Ventura in the halcyon days of flapper fashion...

Art Deco

Gatsby

F. Scott Fitzgerald

The Pierpont Inn was both a hideaway for Hollywood lovers, like Clark Gable and Carole Lombard, Humphrey Bogart and Lauren Bacall, and a retreat for writers. Local attorney Earle Stanley Gardner authored his *Perry Mason* series in his law office down the road from the Inn and actually used it as a backdrop for many of his novels, particularly in "The Case of the Velvet Claws." Silver screen stars, such as Bette Davis, Edward G. Robinson and Charlie Chaplin all took breaks from filming in Hollywood by escaping to the charming location.[35]

The Pierpont Inn is also known for its paranormal activity.

Deceased employees of the inn have been spotted going about their work, only to disappear when confronted. Guests have called down to the front desk to complain about the noise from phantom parties going on in a nearby room. When checked, these rooms were found to be empty.

Perhaps the most famous spirit is the ghost of Emma Darling. Ms. Darling has been a frequent guest at the Pierpont. Apparently she checked in on January 11, 1911 to stay for a serious occasion, perhaps a memorial service, which would explain why her apparition is always seen in somber mourning clothes. She has made her presence strongly known, leaving the unforgettable scent of roses throughout the inn. She has turned the lights off and on, left footprints across the floor, and turned on the gas fireplaces at night. She was a member of the Darling family of Summerland, a town which is well known for its spiritual and paranormal activity.[36]

What would the Great Gatsby have said to Emma?

"Emma, if it weren't for the fog we could see you in the parking lot, dancing by the English Tudor cottages. You always have lights burning all night in your room."

"They see her dancing in the parking lot or they smell her. It's like roses; it's a very distinct scent," says a manager at the inn.

> Apparently when they see her, there is a scent that follows. The reason that I guess she is around is that she was a friend of one of the owners. I guess there are quite a few spirits here at the hotel. A lot of things do happen in this main building. This is the actual building that was the original part of the hotel. This is the one that's a hundred years old. A lot of things do tend to happen upstairs. Somewhere near the copier there's a little storage room. Apparently there's a gentlemen that's in there. I believe they call him Roger, I'm not sure. He's the one I guess who is somewhat irritated or mad. There have been reports of employees being tugged, or they'll feel that coldness, and that usually happens where our coffee machine

is at. It's right next to the storage room. Various psychics were able to come and pinpoint… I guess his name was Roger. There are also little kids that run up and down the hallways, and those are the stories that we hear from our front desk agents. They're here at ten o'clock at night on the late evening shift. They'll hear footsteps or kids running down the hallways. It's late at night, nobody's here, the entire building will be shut down. We do have one bartender who does tend to hear them a lot. He says he's seen one little girl in this storage room down here wearing a yellow dress. The bar closes up around ten or eleven o'clock.

One night I was here with a client, it was late at night. I was talking with her, and I saw him go upstairs. He went to clock out, and I thought I heard something, but I thought it could have been like a semi passing by or something, so I didn't pay no attention to it. And he comes down and he says, 'Hey did you just hear that?' and I said, 'Hear what?' and he said, 'You didn't hear somebody walking across the hallway?' I said, 'Is that what it was? I heard something, but I thought it could have been a truck passing by,' and he said, 'Well, our clocking machine is right upstairs.' He was actually up there and he was clocking out and heard like somebody was running down the hallway, and he looked, but no one was there, but he clearly heard the noises, and I was like maybe it was a semi.

This building has a lot of noises. One morning, I believe I did possibly see something…and that same morning, our director of catering stated that she had seen something as well. She got in about eight o'clock in the morning. When you go upstairs you can clearly see if anyone is in the building, and you have that feeling if you walk up there, if you're by yourself or not. She said she got to work, she was in her office, and she clearly saw a figure walk by her door. It was completely black. We have a controller, she's pretty tall, and she has a black coat and that's who I first thought of; I said, '"Are you sure it wasn't A [name protected]?" And she said, "That's exactly what I thought." She got up and she went to go look.

Looking at A's door, she saw that it was closed, and she knew that nobody was there, and she kind of tried to brush it off like "Maybe I'm just going crazy." And that same evening, I was on the phone and I recall the time—it was about 6:15, around there—and I was talking to somebody and it was funny because I was talking to her about paranormal things at her house because things were happening to her. And as she's talking to me, I see a black figure walk right by the front of my door, and I thought it was the controller, and I was at the point where I was going to yell out, "Thanks for saying goodbye." And so of course I stood up and walked out, but all the doors were closed, and I'm like hmmm. But the funny thing is that I didn't hear any footsteps, and because this is an old craftsmen style building, you'll hear people coming down the hallway, and so the next morning I asked her and she said, "No, I left at 7." I said, "You didn't get up at 6:15 and have a cigarette?" And she said, "I could've, but I just would have gone to the roof over there."

At first I thought it was a person, but after a few seconds I'm realizing... it was weird...that I didn't hear any footsteps, and then I caught myself because I was going to say thanks for saying goodbye, and then I thought that it was kind of weird that I didn't hear any footsteps...and you could tell it was a person, just the way it looked. It was fast, it was too fast, but there were not any footsteps.

In the kitchen some people say that they can hear people saying their name, in the meeting room as well there's a presence that's felt. We did capture a voice in the Vickers estate. An EVP. We heard a voice in the background say, "Yup Yup."

One day a man and his son came in. They wanted to stay in the Vickers Estate. The first night nothing happened. There are three rooms in the Vickers Estate, and you can rent each one. The first night they stayed in, I think it was the Ramona Room, the second night they stayed in 602. Nothing happened. Then they stayed in 601, the Allesandro Room, and apparently the gentleman was so scared he urinated on the bed, and he just left. Most recently it was about two months ago we had a party stay up there, and their claim was that things were being thrown at them. There were coins that kept being thrown at them, and apparently there's some significance because they were all 1986 or something like that. I came in Monday morning and they said, "Oh, something happened this weekend." All of a sudden they're watching TV and something would land on the ground. I'll go up there in broad daylight by myself and sometimes check the rooms, and you do feel kind of creeped out, and I felt that way instantaneously, from the first day I worked here. We do hear a lot of employees say all the time things will fall, lights will turn themselves on all the time. There seems to be more activity when we are renovating. I guess you're disturbing something, opening something up. I think that people have big soft spots in their heart for this hotel. People have gotten married here; they've spent their honeymoon here. I think there's that attachment to it. If that spirit is here, you're changing their concept maybe, so they come and let you know that they're here. I was walking to the Vickers Estate on my second day, and right away I could feel that energy, and it was broad daylight, and they gave me the creeps. I've been in my office late at night, and I feel my back tense up and I got angry. I told them, "You know I'm not here to feel this way, I'm here to help the hotel; my intentions are good for this property; don't do this!" I was mad. I said, "Don't do this to me," and then it literally went away when I started walking down the stairs.

The Pierpont Inn.

> In the hallway leading to the Santa Rosa and San Miguel rooms, they have seen shadowy figures. People were clocking out that night and they could hear people running back and forth. Sometimes I'll be sitting in my chair and my door will be partially open, and I do see my door move every once in a while. This is where I was sitting when I saw the black figure go by. A lot of activity in this general area. We also have the computer room right there, so I'm thinking it's a very high electrical field magnetic area. People who are more sensitive definitely feel more creeped out to that. You can come up here and tell whether you're up here by yourself.
>
> We have some English-style cottages on the property. Actually, George Bush, Sr., stayed in one of our cottages, and I believe the younger George Bush, too. We're definitely going to send them an invitation for the centennial. It's definitely strange because this is the second time this week now I've come to a room and seen it left wide open. Our housekeepers are pretty good. The door is always closed, even if you don't close it all the way, it's not going to swing open. Even if you push it, it doesn't swing open.

It's Sunday, karaoke night at the Pierpont. A woman is belting out "Reminiscing." If you listen carefully between the notes, perhaps you can hear the memories of the spirits past and present at the Pierpont... the weddings, the funerals, the laughter of children. Ventura in its heyday still lives on at the Pierpont, in both the sea and the spirits.

The Pierpont Inn.

THE GHOSTS OF MOORPARK AND THE HISTORIC HAUNTS OF HIGH STREET

(Eleanor) My name is Eleanor. I have haunted this building for many years ... I remember when a toy store and a flower shop resided in this building ...and they began to experience unexplainable, perplexing events. One late evening, the flower shop owner had just finished arranging her stuffed animals in the display window. She locked her store up tight and went home, her eyelids drooping with exhaustion. How surprised she was to open the store the next morning to find a large teddy bear propped at her desk holding a single red rose!

(CW) I overheard employees tell investigators about a woman in a black Victorian dress. They would see her walking back and forth at the top of the staircase, and sometimes, when no one was there, motion detectors would go on and off. Light bulbs would burn out immediately after being replaced, and cupboards would open by themselves ... A female ... with a broken heart... who died of natural causes. She knew she could leave, but she chose to stay. She wanted to remain close to the living, although she still struggles to *really* ... make a connection.

(Z) Well ladies and gentlemen, that's the tale of poor, lonely Eleanor.

(Eleanor) Thank you ... my friends. I shall never forget you.[37]

"Eleanor" is one of the many ghosts that haunt historic High Street in the heart of Moorpark. Every year around Halloween, a group of thespians seeking thrills and chills conduct a tour down High Street, utilizing high drama and theatrical means to introduce guests to the many spirits that have found a permanent residence. The tradition was started by Rosemary Moffat, who has a background in theater, and three other local women. The tour begins and ends at The Secret Garden, a restaurant that is said to be haunted by the spirit of "The Kissing Lady," a woman who was allegedly murdered, after having been promised a part in a play at the theater. She was said to have been killed by two homeless people living in the area at the time. She apparently enjoys kissing the clientele of The Secret Garden on the cheeks.

High Street, The Wardlow Insurance Building, Home of Eleanor.

> **(Kissing Lady)** For behind you (point) is the train which brought me into town. I had the promise of a much-needed role in a musical—right down the street there at the theater—and was walking, alone, on my way there. For just as I was crossing this very street, I saw a handsome gentleman standing right about there (she points) on the site of the Secret Garden today. He was smiling and motioning to me—and I could never resist a good-looking man. Well, just as I got close enough he... he pulled a knife... and he... he... Oh, my friends! I *never* made it to opening night.[38]

An employee at the Secret Garden shared his experience.

The building was built in the early 1900s and used to be the general store of Moorpark for about forty years; that store ended up closing because the local people who picked oranges used the owner of the store to act as a mediator. They went on strike and were complaining against the city and there were some problems, damage to the store...after that, it was a flower shop, a video store, auto body parts shop, ice cream parlor...then the previous owners built the whole building and renovated everything about 12 years ago.

I've heard stories of the lady who took the train who went to apply for a position at the theater; she got off the train the wrong day, and there was no train back home and no hotel, so she was wandering on the street and she was murdered on the street, which is supposedly by the restaurant, and since then her ghost has been floating around.

High Street in Moorpark, The Secret Garden Restaurant.

CROOKED CANDLES

The employee at the Secret Garden continues:

What I have seen at the restaurant is, on the wall by the kitchen, I have two antique-looking candelabra hanging; the candles would be put straight at night, and then a few hours later one would be crooked. I have no idea why that happened; the other three candles are straight; only one was crooked. They were put in there properly. It was like somebody moved them. I cut the wicks of the candles and stopped lighting them because they were leaving a lot of smoke that made black spots on the ceiling, and at one point I had to replace that part of the ceiling. The candles would be there because we had stopped lighting them, and then they started looking crooked. I had no idea why or who did that, meaning it was not an employee who moved the candle, so I have no explanation for it. I melt the bottom of the candelabras to make sure they will be straight; it's something I noticed that was interesting.

Sometimes with one of the chandeliers the light would flicker. Could be the wiring, I don't know, but it doesn't do it all the time. If it was the wiring, it would do it all the time. I did notice that when I was talking to someone, the light flickered. It got dark and light again.

There was something else that was very interesting too with one of my chandeliers. I have dimmers on the light, and I would turn the lights brighter, and all of a sudden they would be dim. Out of nowhere. That was only at night.

Sometimes you would hear door noises, like somebody went to the bathroom? But nobody went to the bathroom. Not like a door shut or opening, but yeah, kind of like a door opening, but not something loud. Just a little bit. Always at night. My waitresses would hear it more than I did; they'd be like, 'Did you hear that?' No customers in the bathroom, no customers in the restaurant, no customers. Not the toilet flush or anything, just like a door; and not the door slamming, just the door closing. So my waitresses are scared to go to the bathroom at night!

The tour continues at the Wardlow Building with the story of Eleanor, and then continues on to The Cactus Patch, a restaurant that is said to house the spirit of Charlie Dorn, a former oilman sporting greasy hands for the ladies' behinds. Throughout the years numerous waitresses have been pinched or grabbed from the behind by phantom hands. There have also been reports from a local psychic who saw Charlie's apparition sitting in his favorite booth at the back of the restaurant!

The tour slips away from Charlie's greasy hands to the corner of High Street to Moorpark's first bank, said to be haunted by Mr. Walter Brennen, a famous character actor. He was best known as Grandpa in the television series, *The Real McCoy's*. The location is now a vaquero store that has experienced various paranormal incidents. Chairs as well as CDs have been moved around the store. A bluish apparition has also been seen standing on the corner in the wee morning hours...

The High Street Arts Center is said to house two entities—Zala the Hungarian Nightingale and Franklin the Construction Chap. A Hungarian singer named Zala was walking down the street dressed in a nice gown when two transients trailed her up to her room and silenced her forever. They say her spirit remains, singing from the balcony or floating across the floor. Zala is not the only residential ghost living in the High Street Theater.

In the 1950s, a construction worker named Frank died while working in the theater, dying under a collapsed steel girder. According to the Script for *The Historic Haunts of High Street,* "They found him the next morning—legs all broken up under him, eyes wide open, mouth stretched into a scream, arms reaching towards the open doorways right there."[39]

The group moves on to the old Moorpark train depot, said to be a vortex where the "Shadow Man" lurks. Elenore, The Kissing Lady, and Zala all join hands to channel a paranormal investigation that occurred last year.

High Street, The Wardlow Insurance Building, Home of Eleanor.

Historic Haunts of Moorpark, Rosemary and Mike Moffat.
Courtesy of Rosemary Moffat

(Eleanor) Souls alive, we mean no harm ... Tell us the cause of your alarm.

(Kissing Lady) Souls alive that breathe the air ... through your eyes, please take us there.

(Eleanor) The psychic can see someone! A shadowy figure of a man! He came out of nowhere!

(Kissing Lady) (Sounding more frightened) Oh my! He is completely void of light ...like a black hole. The investigators are standing in a circle...they are becoming dizzy and they can't breathe.

(Eleanor) The psychic is explaining that the spirit is sucking the energy out of everyone again so he can manifest into visible form again. Apparently two weeks after the investigation the site was torn down, but the spirits of High Street continue to live on.[40]

THE OJAI VALLEY AND SULPHUR MOUNTAIN

Shangri-La was a fictional place described in the novel *Lost Horizon* (1933) as a paradise on earth. It's no surprise that Frank Capra's film version was filmed in the California's Shangri-La, Ojai, a word derived from the Chumash Indians, means "Valley of the Moon."[41][42] The Ojai Valley has always been considered a spiritual and artistic center, and has been the home of such famous residents as Jiddu Krishnamurti, Beatrice Wood, and Aldous Huxley.

As you leave downtown Ojai, the road twists and turns until you reach a straightaway. This is the road leading to Sulphur Mountain, soaring into the sky at a little under 3,000 feet in elevation, famous for its sulphur water source. In the lore of the Chumash Indians, Sulphur Mountain is a bridge between the heavens and earth, and was considered their sacred ground. The peak was considered sanctified by the Avatar of the Age, Meher Baba, who visited Meher Mount on August 2, 1956.[43]

Sulphur Mountain was also said to be the home of the Mountain Chumash Indians, the earliest inhabitants of the Chumash Valley. It is said that the spirits of the Chumash still haunt the mountain. Research indicates that:

> This was a spiritual place for the Indians, and may have been considered as sacred ground. Many people have claimed to have seen full-body apparitions throughout the woods on Sulphur Mountain. People can hear them, people have seen them, and many people have found pictures of ectoplasm on their photographs. When looking at the photographs closer, the ectoplasm at times looks like Indian faces.[44][45]

The Ojai Valley—The View from Sulphur Mountain.

The Ojai Valley—Topa Topa Mountain.

Psychic Louella Diamond spent considerable time on Sulphur Mountain and had various experiences related to the Chumash.

I used to go out to the corner of the cliff. It was so windy and I would find myself being out there for hours. I would look down the inlets and I could see teepees and fires. I would watch them bigger than ants. I could see them walking at night time. I'm not a person that can sit down for three hours at a time and be entertained, but I would become so immersed in these visions, the time would pass without me knowing. I could feel people; not ghosts, but that people were around me; they felt alive but I couldn't see them.

These people were just living here; it wasn't a place they were buried, it was a living area, but they were trying to build a house; they were living their life. A house was being rebuilt that had been burnt down in a fire, in the late 70s. They rebuilt the foundation, but everything that could go wrong went wrong; "It's working fine, it's working great!" An hour later the most bizarre things would happen; the toilet water came into the bathtub that didn't have pipes? How could the toilet water get into a bathtub that didn't have plumbing? And they were putting the walls up, like bricks or siding, and people were sleeping on the foundation; psychic people; they would see wispy apparitions. In the morning where they poured the concrete the sidings would be turned off the plywood. There was one woman who had never seen the outline of a ghost, only the wispy white stuff that a lot of people see; one night she woke up and this ghost was right next to her in outline, and he was trying to move her blankets, and she got up and she looked and she saw a ghost that had some kind of clothes on. The clothing was ambiguous, and she saw him trying to kick the cement and take the plywood from the foundation. She got so scared she left. It always happened around the same time, around 2AM in the morning.

I felt the Chumash spirits didn't want the house to be built. My theory was that they were thinking, "What was this house doing on our land?"

They didn't feel the house was meant to be; I guess they felt their land was being desecrated. I felt like they felt they were still alive, and that they were in between life and death. They needed to go to heaven or return back to life; they were living their lives as spirits. I really don't know how they could be happy like that. They must have had some awakening when the house was built. That people couldn't see them, couldn't talk to them, and weren't abiding by their wishes. I feel like they are little children hiding in the bushes and the parents have left; the Indian children. I can feel them, it's almost like they're frozen in time. It's like I see them and I don't see them...leather tones, golden tones...it's like they were neither alive nor dead.

The Ojai Valley—The View from Sulphur Mountain-Islands in the sky.

The Ojai Valley—The View from Sulphur Mountain.

CHAPTER FOUR

THE PARANORMAL ACTIVITY OF SAN LUIS OBISPO COUNTY

THE PASO ROBLES INN

HELLO? THIS IS J.H., FROM BEYOND THE GRAVE

Below is an excerpt from a charming letter from two elderly guests who spent a very interesting evening at the Paso Robles Inn. The woman begins the letter by thanking the inn for all the amenities one could want, plus one not mentioned. "The GHOST!!"

> About 2:30AM, my husband and I both woke up to the sound of running water. Not the commode, or shower next door, or the hot tub. It was running water in our room, the sound of a jug being filled. As it was filled and was full, the sound quit. Then twice my husband heard the sound of coffee perking. He finally unplugged it so it would quit. The first thing I do when going to bed is to untuck the covers, bedspread, sheets, etc. When we were going to bed after trying to find the source of running water, the bedspread was tucked back in, very neatly. Then the next morning while we were enjoying brunch, the water started running again. Long enough to fill the jug and then quit...while we weren't afraid, it did make for an interesting, albeit, restless sleep for these two old seniors.[46]

The new El Paso de Robles Hotel, now known as the Paso Robles Inn, opened its doors for business in 1891. Solid masonry, set off by sandstone arches, filled the hotel to ensure that it was fireproof. Three stories tall, the new hotel boasted a garden of seven acres, golf course, a library, and billiard rooms. Fifteen years later, in 1906, the Grand Bathhouse was opened. Tiled floors, polished woods, and white marble from Italy made for an elegant experience. Perhaps guests of the inn felt as if they were bathing in an Italian villa. A well on the property produced over two million gallons of mineral water a day.[47]

Such a vast amount of water would have surely come in handy on December 12th, 1940, when this magnificent structure burst into flames.

The fire began at a little past 9PM. A night clerk, J.H. Emsley, discovered the blazes, sounded the fire alarm, and rushed downstairs to alert the guests. Tragically, he died of a heart attack on the spot, the only fatality caused by the fire.

Over the years, the Paso Robles Inn has experienced many types of paranormal activity, with the most famous incident centering on the "ghost caller."

In February 2001, renovations to the ballroom were completed, ushering in a plethora of paranormal activity. On February 1st, 2001, the front desk received mysterious calls from room 1007. When the clerk picked up the phone to answer, there was no voice on the other end. The story really spiced up when 1007 called 911.

"'To dial 911 from the inn's rooms, callers have to hit 8 and 0 before 911," said General Manager Paul Wallace in an article from *The Tribune.* Wallace said the 911 call went out close to 9:05PM, the time Emsley sounded the alarm the night of the fire. Wallace theorizes that Emsley didn't know that the hotel guests were all safely evacuated, and is still trying to alert people. "I think it's unfinished business," Wallace said. "He has no idea that the 200 guests were escorted out safely." Wallace has no idea why the ghost chose 1007 to make his calls. But he noted that that part of the hotel was built with bricks from the original hotel. "Maybe they somehow carried Emsley's spirit with them."[48]

"He never knew everybody got out. That's how we connected the 911 calls," says an employee of the hotel.

> He is still trying to get people out of the hotel. This was just last week. M [name protected] was in 1007 and the phone rang; he picked it up and there was nothing there, just static. It was on hold but it called us. Two different phone systems. This is a brand new phone system. I talked to the technician who worked on our old phone system. It was an old Lexcar phone system, and I asked

him specifically if there was any way possible this phone could freak out and call 911, and he told me there was no way that could physically happen. 911 twice. The fact that it dialed every extension on the property. He came and looked into the system; he couldn't figure out why it was doing that. And then it starts happening on this brand new phone system. We just got this installed six months ago, and now it's starting to happen on this system too, the same room. Someone calls the police station saying there's a fire and there's no one staying in the room. They've heard a voice speaking.

In February 2001, one more piece was added to the paranormal puzzle. *The Pacific Coast Business Times* reported in its February issue:

In the local paper that reported Emsley's death was a letter from a bellhop. The hotel bellhop blamed the fire on a black cat that had showed up at the hotel and had been staring in at them. Now there's an entire family of black cats living just behind the resurrected ballroom.[49]

California Hauntspitality also reported around the same time:

The ballroom is the only remaining portion of the original building not destroyed by the 1940 fire. The present-day cats seem to have a tie to the original building. According to a newspaper article recently unearthed by management, on December 17, 1940, a bellman reported seeing a black cat in the lobby. The employee was convinced that the cat was a portent of something bad. Two days later on December 19th, 1940, a devastating fire engulfed all but the ballroom, and claimed the life of J.H. Emsley who died in the lobby where the cat was sighted. Why are the cats showing up now?"[50]

Another employee has had her own share of paranormal events.

The security cameras and videos. When I started, I noticed one; there's this little orb, and it's always there, and it never moves. Like people can walk through it and it shows on the screen back there, and one night M and I were standing in the back, and I heard someone come in the door, and no one had come in the door, and when I looked at the screen my little orb moved, and it's never moved since, and it's never moved before, and when I put my arm out it feels cold. Yeah, I call him Fred, like a little light. I was shocked.

The Paso Robles Inn.

The Paso Robles Inn. Ballroom.

The Paso Robles Inn. Room 1007.

One night I was here and I thought it was G up in the bar, and he comes walking in this way. Hoof! It sounded like there were people talking up in the bar and nobody was up there. It was probably 11 o'clock, and I thought it was G up there checking because he walks around, our night security guy, and I was about to call him and he comes walking in this door, and it's like G. I asked, "Were you up in the bar?" and he's all "No." And at night after you guys leave, the radios. You can hear the radios key up, and I know that everyone's gone. After ten. It's happened a couple of times.

One guest said that when they came back to their room one time, all of their amenities were sitting next to their bed. In the 7s (room 700). I have heard stories in the 6, 7 and 8s. I have had people tell me they'll wake up in the morning and the water bottle was empty next to the bed, and they didn't drink anything out of the water bottle.

In Room 303, there was a guest who was staying by himself. He said that he woke up in the middle of the night to a strange noise. He remembers that his chair was pushed in to the desk. His shoes and socks were right next to the chair. When he woke up in the middle of the night after hearing the strange noise, the chair was pulled out and turned to the side like somebody had pulled it out and sat in it, and his shoes were completely tipped over. His socks were spread out—and he was completely by himself. Nobody else had the key to his room. He reported that to us in the morning. This happened the beginning of November 2009. Some of our tenants would get random phone calls from other guests in the middle of the night. We always think they're from 1007. Dead air, like somebody was there on the other line, but not talking...

PARANORMAL EVENTS RECORDED IN MAY AND JUNE OF 2001.

- Room 402—Lights off and on, water vanished
- Room 1209—TV off and on, flash by mirror in the hallway
- Room 1202—Someone's cell phone disappeared
- Room 806—Guest asked, "Is this place haunted?"
- "An employee was coming to work in the morning and he saw a female apparition standing on the bridge there. He went to

approach her and she was gone. That happened twice to him and he quit. It was early in the morning, about 6AM. He was a cook."

The Paso Robles Inn. Bridge where a ghost was seen.

Another employee relates her story.

I was in the lounge really late one night. I was counting money and I felt somebody or something behind me, like watching. You know how you feel that? So I looked, and said, "Oh, I'm almost done." We had the old-fashioned time clock, and I had just cleaned the counter and put some pennies on it, and right then the pennies rolled on the ground. I heard them, they were in the other room. There's no way they could have... and so I left, took the money in the bag. A black cat ran in front of my car when I pulled out of the driveway.

> The two stories of the little girl in room 1212 were when a couple checked in 6PM. At 2AM they came down to the front desk and said they had to leave. Our night clerk asked, "Why?" and they said because the wife woke up and there was a little girl standing at the edge of the bed, and she couldn't figure out why this little girl was in the room. The little girl went into the bathroom and the wife got up to find out what this little girl was doing in the room, and the little girl was gone. The next one was when I heard about three weeks ago when the wife woke up and the little girl was standing at the foot of the bed, and then she just turned and disappeared. The other stories are that the other people see the girl in the hallway, usually down at the end. As they approach her or as they're watching her, she'll turn and go into a room. There are multiple stories from many different people. She's not like an apparition, or a fog or a mist you can see through, or a shadow. They see facial features, they see what she's wearing; her bow in her hair. The housekeeper identified her as the little girl from the book we keep at the front desk. *The History of the Paso Robles Inn.* On page 74 there is a black and white photo of a little girl standing next to her brother, feeding turkeys.

A trip to the Paso Robles Historical Society revealed her to be Mary Elizabeth Sawyer. The ghosts of children are usually associated with trauma and an early death. Yet further research at ancestry.com led to the revelation of Mary boarding a ship for Japan at the age of twenty-one. This discounts the theory of Mary dying as a young girl, and thus turning into a "ghost."

"There are plenty of ghosts of people who are still alive. This is my theory," says paranormal investigator, Richard Senate. "An event took place a long time ago when this person was a little girl. It was a very stressful event. She could have been running from an abusive parent. She could have been molested. When she ran down that hallway she left something behind, an emotional imprint, and under the right atmospheric conditions, and the right psychological situation, it can replay."

The employee continued:

The 1200s. W [name protected] and I, we were the only two up there. I have a pet peeve thing about those doors being closed because my housekeepers at night time said that's where they see the little girl, so we did a few rooms, and then W and I went downstairs. When we came back up, one of the doors, the swinging doors, were open to the ice machine upstairs. I looked at W and remember telling him, "I hate them being open so I shut them." And I said, "If this happens again you're doing this on your own." M said that she was going upstairs, and she felt two little hands on her back, and that was in the back stairwell. She turned around and there was nobody there. On another night in the laundry room A [name protected] and M were both working one night, and A was in the bathroom. She was cleaning the corner and M was doing laundry. She felt somebody tap on her and say, "V" which is V's [name protected] nickname (the other housekeeper.) She heard a little girl's voice. She turned around and asked M if she said anything, and she said no. They both identified her in the book. She said the little girl looks just like that.

I've heard stories from guests that the water has been on the right night stand, and the next morning, when they woke up, it was on the left night stand. I've heard stuff being moved around in the bathrooms. 6, 7 and 8s, the water bottle being moved around in the rooms; that's an older part of the hotel from 1941. After the fire; the whole thing is, the bricks are from the original building. Everyone says that can carry the paranormal activity left in the bricks. The 10s and 11s are where I had the phone calls; that's brand new. That's built on the site of the old bathhouse.

See, the paranormal activity that usually happens is like this: When we start some kind of construction somewhere, we get all this activity going on. Right now we're doing construction. We tore down this old bank building that's been around for years. We're gonna build a bathhouse, and about that time started is when... The only time that it didn't start is with the little girl in the ballroom, that's been going on for years now. People see her up there. One of the housekeepers saw her up in the ballroom and came downstairs. The third housekeeper that night actually had someone touch her. This is the same little girl that a guest actually saw in the room with her. 1208 or 1209. That was built in about 1912. The second story was added in 1912. It's not an apparition or something you can see through, it's a solid little girl. The guests that saw her in the room checked in at 6PM and came down at 2AM, and had to leave because the wife woke up and the girl was standing next to the bed. The building where she was seen was the crews' quarters, where the help stayed. There are 16 rooms up there. The shower turning on when there was nowhere in the room, and the voices of children running down the hallway in the crews' quarters.

The Paso Robles Inn. Hallway of the little girl.

THE INTERDIMENSIONAL UNIVERSE

INTERVIEW WITH PARANORMAL RESEARCHER AND AUTHOR RICHARD SENATE

What exactly are ghosts? Do they exist in other realms in the universe?

The question is not whether ghosts exist or not, but what is their nature? Paranormal researcher and author Richard Senate has been trying to answer this question for the last twenty years. He says:

> Ghosts transect the scientific and metaphysical worlds, and give hints at a post-death experience. Religion and faith mix with science and skepticism—when it comes to the question of ghosts and haunted places—it's a difficult quest. We need to take ego out of the mix. Too many ghost hunters have egos the size of opera singers. The same goes for psychics.[51] I believe we need to blend the psychic impressions with readings collected by tools. We, as groups will need to work together if we are to make this newest of sciences become recognized. There is far too much in-fighting going on now. We must work together.[52] The dead do not die. Now that we have passed beyond the Newtonian world view of the universe as a giant pocket watch, It's good to see views that have a place for the paranormal world.

While working as an archaeologist at the old Spanish Mission of San Antonio de Adua in King City, California, Richard Senate saw a monk with a candle. When he approached the monk he vanished.

> It didn't look like a ghost one sees in TV or film—it looked like a real guy up until it vanished away. I later learned others had seen him, and there were many ghost stories there.[53]

It was from this first ghostly encounter that Richard Senate began a career of paranormal research that has spanned over two decades. He grew up in Los Angeles, where his father worked for MGM studios and his mother as a housewife. The family moved to the Ventura area in 1952, where Richard lived most of his life.

> For twenty-two years I was the historian of Ventura. I retired in 2005, but I still do tours for the city. I've always been involved in ghosts,

and that came about when I was doing archaeology. One night I saw a ghost at one of the old California missions, San Antonio, near King City, and it was so unexpected and profound, it got me involved in the study of ghosts. I've been doing it ever since, not only in southern California, but in Arizona, Nevada, Hawaii, England, New Orleans… a variety of different places. I've had seventeen books published now. I've consulted on a number of TV shows, from *In Search of Haunted Hollywood*, to things like *Sightings* and *Haunted Hotels*, and most recently *Dead Famous.*

In all of my quests, I really don't have as many answers as I'd like. In fact, every time I try to find an answer, I usually open up more questions about what things might be. In all my years of work, which is now thirty years, I've found a couple of patterns. Buildings that have lots of natural material, like stone, tend to be haunted, or adobe; the *thickness* of the walls seems to lend itself to it, so you find European castles, cathedrals, all that. It seems like the materials might focus the energy. Also, places tend to be haunted where there's a colorful history, where people undergo great stress. Like battlefields.

The courthouse in Ventura, people were tried there, and that's a very stressful thing. Also, we find that churches are haunted and schools, also places where people faced execution. Mental hospitals, regular hospitals. These places exhibit patterns of stress.

Richard Senate.

As I said before, there are plenty of ghosts of people who are still alive. I knew a psychic up in Sacramento, and she knew of a mansion, and she was walking in the mansion and there was a mirror, and in the mirror she saw a man. The man was standing there, trembling, and she looked but there was no person to reflect the image, so she finally figured it out. "I think I've seen a ghost." And wouldn't you know, about six months later she met the man who was in the mirror, and he worked in the same building. So she got to talking with him, and she told him what she had seen, and this is what he told her: He had divorced his wife and she took him to the cleaners, and she had gotten a very young husband to replace him. He was invited to the mansion to go to this gala opening, as he was a very influential member of the community. So he went in and saw his wife and her new husband laughing and talking together, and it got him so insanely jealous and upset he had to leave, but that emotional imprint got stuck there in the mirror, and it replayed. I don't think it accounts for all ghosts, but for some of them. There are things out there that we may not be able to detect, but are there just the same. I believe that it has to do with the nature of reality itself. I think that a lot of things that people see are simply time slips, but they're also just plain old-fashioned real ghosts too; so many stories. Even my own family. You know how many stories I get of widows who have seen their spouses? About eighty-five percent; now some of that's wishful thinking, but not all of it. And you know what's cool? They usually leave a message and the message is always the same—"I'm okay. Everything is all right."

It's like the death camps in Europe. You can always see ghosts, and it's usually not the people who died in the gas chambers, but the guards. I think guilt has a lot to do with it. The missions are all haunted and who haunts them? Not the natives who suffered so much, but the padres—they're the ones who are there. I tend to think that time spins. I think that there are alternate realties. Way over there is a duplicate of us, and in that dimension there's a whole different world. The very fact that we can think of a scenario signifies that it probably exists somewhere. I compare ghost hunting to walking on Jell-O. We have theories, but few answers. Few facts, but I do have a few facts—places with stress are haunted. Places with a death experience tend to be haunted, and every hospital is haunted. Nursing homes—and I've talked to so many nurses who have been with patients just before they die, and they're very alert and talkative and happy. Not sad but happy.

And they usually say "Last night my mother came to visit me," but the lady is eighty-eight years old. Many times when people do pass away, they'll see their loved ones come for them. Their mother, their father, husband, etc...and doctors will see a shadow and the patient will say, "Oh Harold, where have you been?" and then they die. That's such a great thought, to know that when our day comes, there will be someone to take us to wherever we go.

The Ojai Valley may be a vortex or portal. I believe there are areas where the psychic gifts of people are enhanced. It could be discharges of electromagnetic energy. Earthquakes discharge electromagnetic energy, and we pick this up subconsciously and it enhances our ability, so it gives us the chance to see the ghosts. They're always here, and I've seen there are particular streets where there are many ghost sightings. Ojai, even stories from the skeptics, so it's not just being attuned to it, but it also maybe has something to do with the environment. That's just a theory. The Chumash were, and still are, a very psychic people. Many of the native peoples are. Remarkably many of the Chumash are devout Catholics. Some of them are more Catholic than the Pope. What they did was take their native beliefs and Christian beliefs, and blended them.

Ghosts are but a footprint upon the sands of time. If you undergo a great trauma, it will leave something behind, like a footprint and under the right circumstances, could be the weather, it will hit just right and you will relive that moment, or you'll see something from that other time. A footprint or a replay, like a video tape of a past event. I tend to think that time might be the key to much of this. For a number of people who see ghosts, usually the ghosts are not interacting with them, they're just there. Kind of like you stumbled into them, so I think that might well be a snippet from the past. Some ghosts do interact with you, some ghosts *have even saved people's lives.* A classic case: A young lady is going with her friends to Las Vegas. She's packing her bag and hears her grandfather's ghost say: "Don't go." Her grandmother came up and said, "I heard grandpa say don't go," so she went to her friends and said, "Sorry, I'm not gonna go with you." They were sad, but they drove off. Wouldn't you know they got into a terrible accident. The car hit the vehicle and smashed that whole side of the car where she would have been seated. This girl was from the east end of Ventura.

Here's a story I got from a lady who is a bank manager from New Jersey. Her brother liked taking drugs and motorcycles, and he was a good mechanic. One night she was asleep and she saw the door open. She saw a blue light in the bedroom. It was her brother and he had a blue motorcycle, and he had been killed on the very night this thing happened, and the same exact thing happened to her sister in New York. In another story, a lady had a sister who was always sick. Young, nice, but she had this terminal illness. She got a call saying her sister was in the hospital in Houston, Texas I think it was, and they didn't expect her to live, so she got leave from her company and flew back to Texas. She worked for a chemical company in Thousand Oaks. She flew in and called from the airport. They told her that her sister had recovered, and that she would be coming home. She said, "Well, I'll come anyway." So she's on the plane to Texas and she looks out the window and she sees her sister's face on the outside of the plane looking in, and then it disappears. Well she came down and no one was there to pick her up. Finally, she got a taxi and went home. Another relative told her the sister was dead. She had had a sudden relapse. The thing that was funny was the point she died was the same time she saw the face outside the plane. Stories like this are common.

It happened to my family. My wife's father had been sick. One night my wife woke up and said that dad had been there. He had said, "I'm here to say goodbye." Now it's snowing outside. She puts on her robe and slippers and runs to his house down the street, knocks on the front door, and she asked, "Is dad okay?" And the lady said, "I haven't checked him since four o'clock." They went into the living room where he had been sleeping and he was dead. The doctors said he must have passed about five-ten minutes before because he was still warm, and that would be about the same time she had the experience.

What About the Carl Jung Quote: "Why Should There Not Be Ghosts?"

When I started this work thirty years ago, ten percent of people believed in ghosts. Now it's more like thirty to forty percent. I think that people who are spiritual believe in some form of life after death and in spirit contact, through angels, ghosts. I think more than half believe there is something out there.

DO YOU THINK THAT WE'LL HAVE A CLEARER UNDERSTANDING OF DEATH ONCE PEOPLE EMBRACE THE PARANORMAL MORE?

Say you don't believe in ghosts and then you see one. What are your options? You have been tricked somehow, or you're insane. Those are your only two options if you don't believe in ghosts. Now, if you believe in ghosts and you see one, what are your options? Well it could be the same, you might be hallucinating, or you might have actually seen a ghost! And many times, ghostly sightings make people become better and rethink their point of view, and maybe even reevaluate their lives. People have a supernatural experience and become more spiritual and open minded, so the way I think of it, it's not a negative, but positive experience. Gypsies are the greatest thieves who ever lived, but are there any gypsies who killed someone? No. They don't believe in it. Part of the belief system is a firm belief in ghosts, and if you killed someone, the ghost would come back to seek revenge. I believe if more people believed in ghosts there would be fewer murders and crimes, because if you believe in ghosts, there are no perfect crimes. The victim would come back for you.

CAN YOU PLEASE EXPLAIN ABOUT RETROCOGNITION? WHAT IS THAT EXACTLY?

Retrocognition is literally, briefly, stepping back into time. Most retrocognitive events are short. We're talking minutes or seconds. A classic case: British Society for Psychical Research, 1952. A lady went to a drugstore—England, London. She walked in and found it full of soldiers in uniforms, and smoke was coming out, like a bar! She goes, "What the heck?" She walked outside and looked at the sign and it said, "Apothecary Shop." She walked back in, and it was a drugstore. She reported, they investigated it. That building had been used as a canteen for soldiers in 1944. Literally, she went from 1952 and stepped into 1944! And then stepped back again. These are really kinds of common things that happen. The most bizarre case is in the great palace of Versailles, where numerous people over the years have retrocognitive events. Two ladies ended up walking though the garden for two hours conversing in French, wearing tri-quad hats. They thought it was a pageant, then when they were done and went back through the garden, there were just plowed fields. It had all been torn out during the French Revolution. They had skipped back to the eighteenth century. A guy was in the great palace and there was a barrier saying, "Do not go beyond this point," and he wanted to get a good picture. A guy came up dressed as a guard from the eighteenth century and told him to leave! And he thought, *well, maybe they're in costume today.*

I may have had one. I went to one of the old missions, La Purísima, and briefly I got like this flash. Just a few seconds, where I saw Native American people, all this stuff, and then it was gone. Well, what amazed me was that I'm a mission historian, but what I saw was different from what I had been told. I just recently found out that my vision or whatever it was, was more accurate, and then it all vanished.

Then there is the battlefield at Gettysburg, where people have not only seen ghosts, but interacted with them. One ghost actually took a picture of a family. They were out there visiting the battlefield and one guy came up dressed as a confederate soldier, took the camera away and took a picture of them. They took pictures of him, too. When they developed them, there was nothing there, just a blank space where he should have been, and they could tell from the insignia he was wearing that he was from a particular regiment in Texas, and that regiment had almost been annihilated on that site defending the territory. He always asks who won the Civil War. When people say the north won, he disappears. Oddly enough, a guy named Nesbit [Mark Nesbit], I know his cousin, has written several books on the ghosts of Gettysburg, but I think that it's one of those spots where you find time of then and now come close.

I was doing a radio show, and a lady called in and told me this experience. There is a road down here, San Jon, which means "ditch," in Spanish. This lady's daughter worked as a cocktail waitress. Her mother had her sister visiting from back east. They chatted until 2:30AM, and then got in the car to go pick up the daughter at 2:30 at night. They were driving along when everything kind of disappeared. Each of the three ladies said they got kind of an upset stomach. A headache. Everything briefly became two dimensional. The trees looked like they were painted of cardboard; not three dimensional, but two dimensional. That's the same thing the ladies reported at Versailles. They got up to the street where it joins the other street, which is Thompson. They stop at the light; the light's red, 2:30AM at night. They saw a car going down Thompson Boulevard. When it got closer, they saw it had no wheels. In fact, it was the weirdest car they ever saw. It had one continuous windshield that went from the front of the car all the way to the back, and it made no sound, just kind of floated right past them and disappeared; and they asked: Was this a ghost? Was it a UFO or who knows what? I think they were looking at some sort of future world where cars without wheels might exist. San Jon, that particular spot might be a vortex.

SO WHEN YOU TALK ABOUT GHOSTS AS RELATED TO TIME, DO YOU THINK THAT GHOSTS COULD BE FROM THE FUTURE? OR COULD THEY BE FROM THE PAST?

Yes. Ghosts are more likely from the past, but they could be from the future too. It may be remarkable, but we may be ghosts. We might be sitting here, and this building might be a nightclub in the year 5050. People might see us sitting here… Well, it's just us. We're not haunting the place, but our energy for some reason…when we have communicated with ghosts and with psychic mediums and such… One thing that seems to be consistent is that they don't seem to be aware of time. When we were at the Santa Maria Inn, there was a ghost there and we found out she had killed herself in 1934. We asked her what year it was. She said 1936. In her frame of reference, two years had passed. In truth it had been decades.

The first ghost I saw, a monk was walking through a corridor and he disappears. My question is: Where did he go? What happened? I think he skipped through time. Here we are on Thursday. I see the ghost. He jumped into Friday. Now of course I can't follow him, so from my point of view he disappeared, but from the ghost's point of view, I disappeared. He's still in the same spot, just in a different time. Ghosts might be able to skip time, which would account for places that were very haunted, no activity, and then haunted again because we're skipping through time. It might also handle stories of reports, things that disappear. You look and look and there's nothing there, and then a week later they seem to reappear. A ghost could pick something up and then take it with them. They tend to operate not on our time frame, and I think we tend to make a mistake. We tend to think of them as people without bodies, but not true. I think the logical part is diminished. All they are made up of are emotions, wrapped up in hate, love...think about this—why do ghosts come back? All emotional reasons, love, to see how a grandchild is doing, hate, to get revenge on someone. Real or imagined. All of these are the last things that they would have done. An unfulfilled wish. Ghosts are emotional traces, and I think that's what we get so much of. In fact, when we do communicate with ghosts, we tend to not get a full personality, but a partial personality. Remember *The Three Faces of Eve?* It's like a person dies, and one fragment is left behind. The rest goes on to wherever it's supposed to go. They are running around with this one single thought. This is the haunting. When you talk to ghosts, they tend to be monogamous. Talking about one thing over and over again. The circular thought or behavior. I tend to think that emotion has a lot to do with what we call a "ghost."

COULD IT BE THAT THIS THINNING OUT OF THE EMOTIONAL TRACE OR "GOING TO THE LIGHT" IS ACTUALLY THE RELEASE OF THE GHOSTS EMOTIONS? AND IS IT POSSIBLE FOR GHOSTS TO SEE US?

I think that ghosts can see us sometimes, and sometimes they don't. These ghosts that are linked to time, they're like a video tape; they don't see us. They're some that do. In the haunted house that we lived in, in the garage, the lady had hung herself. The garage was cold. The dogs we had would not go in there, and over time, she would toss things around. We'd see apparitions, and it got to the point where it only happened in the month of February, which was the month that she died in, and she had dogs too, so she liked our dogs. On the whole, she seemed to be happy. When we finally had to move, she hated it. She would lock the front door and set the deadbolt. We didn't even have a key to the deadbolt. When the real estate agent would come, the door would be locked. She would lock the deadbolt. Finally, he got so angry he took the deadbolt out, and we moved, and the next week he had a buyer. The deadbolt wouldn't let him in, but the deadbolt was gone. The ghost didn't want us to leave. If you have a ghost, talk to them. Give them a name.

HOW CAN GHOSTS MAKE SOUNDS LIKE FOOTSTEPS IF THEY ARE JUST APPARITIONS?

First, the question is, how we do we hear sounds? By hearing vibrations with our ears. It could be that ghosts don't operate that way. They go directly to our minds. When we see a ghost, we may not be seeing a collective light like we see with our minds. We might be seeing it with our mind's eye. It maybe skipping over our senses, going directly to our cognizant being. Our own minds are what we're getting, so that might explain why when you have three people in the room, two will see a ghost and one person will see nothing. Maybe they're not receptive enough to pick it up, but it's not something that exists in "real space." It's something that exists on some other psychic level.

Here's the story I like to tell. There's a funeral home in town, and they called me and said their cemetery office was haunted. They had an old guy working there in the records, and he had retired, but then when they got behind, they called him briefly to help clean up the records. He had a little office in the back wall. Well, he died of a massive heart attack, but they would see him come to work and go into his office. So I said, "'Okay, well I'll get my team of people together and see what we can do," but then they said, "Sorry, you can't do that; the people who own the cemetery are born again Christians." So I was left with a dilemma, how could I help them? So I told them to build a shrine to the man. He may not know he's dead. A death notice, pictures of him, "We'll miss you Charlie," things that he liked, flowers, candles, etc. So they did; they built this little monument with a big cross, his obituary and his picture, everything. They hung it is his office. The owner saw it and said, "What's this?" "Well, we miss our friend Charles." When they did that, they saw the ghost only one more time, in the lobby going into this office. He went into the back where his office was. They never saw him again, so maybe he read materials, realized he was dead, and then went to wherever he was supposed to go.

Ever wonder why they put those crosses along the side of the road? They say when someone has an accident, the trauma is so bad the ghost has amnesia and can't recall the horrific situation that ended their lives, so they don't know they're dead, so they put up the cross so the poor ghost can see it and say, "I'm dead, maybe that's why no one's paying attention to me!"

We had a lady up the road, her house was haunted and she was afraid her children would be afraid of the ghost lady. An elderly woman was seen sitting in the kitchen. She poured the ghost a cup of tea: one for her and one for the ghost, and she addressed the empty chair. She said, "Well you know you're dead, and I don't want you to frighten my children. Please don't scare them, they wouldn't understand. You're welcome to live in the kitchen, but I just wanted to let you know you're dead." She told me that if that cup had moved and trembled she would have been out the door, but they never saw the ghost again.

I also feel that ghosts feed on emotions. The people who live in the haunted homes are going through some kind of emotional stress. Someone lost their job, etc., and this emotional stress might stimulate some kind of stuff. The theory is that ghosts take energy from the living, like batteries, to manifest themselves, and I think there might be something to it. At the Olivas Adobe I saw this dang ghost of a little girl, and she was seen over and over again. A guy came with a camera to take a picture of her, so he was there, and we were upstairs and he would call out her name and she would appear. Pretty consistent too. Finally he called her name out and he was taking a picture. All of his batteries went dead. She was just a fuzzy form. She was taking the energy from the batteries of the camera and using it. A lady had a cell phone and that battery went dead too, and this is consistent over and over again, especially in poltergeist cases. We were investigating a poltergeist case and every time we tried to get a picture? The batteries would go dead. My advice was to get an old camera, the kind that uses gears, like a World War II wind up 16 mm camera, then get special "candlelight" film, and load it up with that. They tried it and they actually got the apparitions on camera. Ghosts can manipulate electronics.

It's not in our realm. It's not like it's going directly onto the film or onto the matrix of the electronic camera. It's being manipulated directly into the electric field. We tend to think of ghosts like us, they're not like us; they're a different kind of thing. I don't have all the answers, I wish I did. There's a lot more work that needs to be done. We need a new science and we need to call it "phantomology." Parapsychologists get involved in telepathy and mind control. I think we need just a science or study to involve just the haunted ghosts. Not get into UFOs, etc., just this *one limited subject.*

IS THERE ANY SCIENTIFIC PROOF THERE ARE GHOSTS? THERE HAS BEEN A LOT OF TALK OF THE RELATIONSHIP BETWEEN THE PARANORMAL AND QUANTUM PHYSICS.

I don't know, but I think we're getting close because we've developed very sensitive pieces of equipment that can pick things up.

We're getting a lot more video tapes of ghost, not all of them are fake. There are fakes out there, but I think that we are getting closer to that dream. Something that we can conclusively prove. Unfortunately, a lot of these people who are doing ghost hunting rely on these very, very sensitive pieces of equipment, but they are so eager to get a blip or a beep that might be a ghost, they're forgetting how much of this world we are in is filled with electronics. TVs and computers and microwaves, they're everywhere. I talked to this one lady, "Oh, I was standing right here and got a reaction." It was right by the electrical plug. Yeah, she was getting a reaction, but it was only from a naturally occurring power source. This is why when you go somewhere like an adobe or a cold building where there isn't a lot of electricity you may get something real. It's kind of like UFOs; we've shot so much junk into space, you might think that you've seen a UFO, but it might just be a Russian satellite coming at you. It doesn't mean there's a spaceship from another planet. I think partly that's where we fell apart with all of our equipment, is that we might be picking up a ghost or we might be picking up any number of other things.

BUT DON'T YOU THINK THAT EVPS (ELECTRONIC VOICE PHENOMENA) ARE ACTUAL PROOF?

Only if it's a good EVP. There's a bunch of bad EVPs. True story. A guy called me up; this is when the Scott Peterson story was big. He went to the place where they got the body and he said he got an EVP. It said: "Scott killed me." So he actually drove down to Ventura from San Francisco, set up his equipment and said, "Here, listen to it," and it went (blurb blurb). Play it again. (blurby). It didn't say anything; he just imagined it said, "Scott killed me." I like EVPs, but only when they're understandable and you can get three people in a room and you push a button and they all agree on what's being said. It's not something you superimpose onto the sound, and I don't like EVPs that have been manipulated. Good EVPs are solid.

DO YOU THINK THAT ALL HUMAN BEINGS HAVE A PHYSICAL BODY AND A SPIRITUAL BODY?

That's a possibility. I won't say that I completely believe in that. I do believe that gases and things do leave a body when they die, and

I do believe there is a spiritual side, and that there is some essence of a person that exists after their death. I don't know if I buy into the theological parts of it, but I think that's true. I think there's definitely something that remains but, I'm not ready to say there's a spirit person. Some of the metaphysicians say that's how it is. Well, I want more information. A good percentage of the ghosts seen are recognized as people who aren't dead. Forty percent. "Oh, that's Aunt Jane," only to discover that Aunt Jane isn't dead yet. What we see could be looking back and forth in time. Aunt Jane will come over for a visit in a month. You were simply looking into the future when that event would happen, or you were looking back into the past when that event occurred, when she came by for a visit. So it might be that, as opposed to her spirit, or it could have something to do with telepathy. I do believe that if someone is thinking about someone, their mind can pick up on that thought.

DO GHOSTS EXIST IN OTHER DIMENSIONS?

That's one of the theories about ghosts, that they're interdimensional beings. In this theory there are other dimensions, and in those dimensions are replicas of us. They exist in that world. People see ghosts of themselves, and there are many accounts of ghosts walking through walls. After doing a historical study, what they actually went through was once a door. They're walking on the floor of the past through a door that no longer exists. That might account for it, but there's a number of things that don't quite jell with that theory either. When you see a ghost go through a wall, it's actually walking through a psychic door, a door that existed in that spot in the past. No one really knows what ghosts are. I believe that we're all living creatures, made up of energy. Wherever we go, we leave that energy behind. The haunting type ghosts are like a roll of film being played over and over.

SO YOU MEAN WHEN YOU SEE A GHOST THAT WALKS THROUGH A WALL (IN OUR DIMENSION) THAT COULD MEAN THAT COULD HAVE BEEN A DOORWAY IN THEIR DIMENSION?

Yes. Their house is different from ours. Okay, a guy did some studies on astral projection, and they found over and over again, a guy would lay down, go into a trance, leave his body, and they would set up a target somewhere, and the idea would be for the guy to leave his body, go find the target, and then come back and describe what he's doing, and it was very successful. But in every occasion something was off. For example, he would describe a fireplace with a painting over it. He would say the painting was a horse, but actually it was a sailing ship. The theory was that they weren't really traveling out of their body, but going into the next dimension, and in that dimension the guy had a horse instead of a sailing ship, but there were people like us in that dimension. So it could be there are other dimensions and we can travel briefly between them, or see images from that other dimension.

COULD YOU EXPLAIN THE THEORY OF PARALLEL DIMENSIONS IN MORE DETAIL?

Okay, well think of it this way. You're here and there's another vibration level that is an exact duplicate of this world, but slightly different. In that world, you're wearing your blue coat and not your black coat. Maybe I'm wearing my gray shirt. Maybe things are just a little bit different. In that dimension, John McCain is the president, and then beyond him there's another dimension, and it's just like this dimension, and even slightly different, and another dimension and another, hundreds of them. It's like a mirror reflecting back and forth, thousands this way and thousands that way. We're just in one and we're living our lives like we're the only one. The reality is that there are all these parallel dimensions and they spin off. New ones as great events happen. There's one over there where the twin towers are still standing.

WHEN WE'RE TALKING TO GHOSTS, ARE WE TALKING IN THE SAME DIMENSION?

Yes, or maybe they're from another dimension, but they're visiting. The whole theory is that UFOs might be interdimensional vehicles. Some people go from here to there, but there are duplicates of us in all these other realms.

I think you have a fascinating project, and you'll end up with more questions than answers. It's like walking on Jell-O. There are very few firm rules. It's all speculation and metaphysical. I talked to one lady and she asked me, "Why you are doing this?" She said we have all the answers, and I asked her, "What are ghosts?" and she said, "Ghosts are the third astral body. We have this shell around us, and when we die this third body stays behind." I said, "Okay, that's a good theory, where did you get it?" "Oh, Madame *so and so* went into a trance." "Oh, where did she get it from?" "Oh, someone from Atlantis."

Now, I'd like to be able to check on someone from Atlantis. So there are a lot of theories, a lot of speculation but few facts, so it's frustrating. The only thing I can say is don't narrow yourself to one belief. Keep your mind open. Follow wherever the truth leads. It may lead you somewhere you don't want to go but follow it anyway. Too many people stick themselves to a theory, and then this doesn't fit, so they try so hard to pound and make it fit. Don't do that. I don't think the answer is so cut and dry. I don't think that all ghosts are spirits of the dead, but a few might be. I don't think they are all videotapes on the fabric of time, but some might be. Anything is possible. The dimension of ghosts—their existence point is very different from ours. Their time is different. Now I don't know how valid this is, but the ghosts can *hear* color, they can *see* sound. Human beings are, as one ghost said, "Glowing Jell-O." Like reddish energy. Like a person, but it doesn't have the body that we know of. This was through a medium. I asked him, "What do we look like?" "Well, you look like glowing Jell-O."

CAN YOU EXPLAIN WHY GHOSTS SOMETIMES MANIFEST AS ORBS OR LIGHT AS OPPOSED TO APPARITIONS?

I think it has to do not so much with the ghosts, but with the person perceiving. They might not be able to process so much data. All they can process is that light. We don't know; as I said there's a lot of mystery involved here, but we do know there are patterns, and these are recurring over and over again. I think it's a good idea to look at what's been done in the past. It's good because you'll notice the same stories being told over and over again, and you'll be able to figure out what's real and what's not, just by the repetition of it. I asked D.

Scott Rogo, one of the great paranormal people out there. Phone calls from the dead. What should we say to skeptics? And he answered: "Look at the literature out there. For over a hundred years we've been collecting data. All this material, all those events. All of these people weren't drunk or crazy." All this material indicates at least a portion of it is credible, it's true. If just one ghost story is true, it means that ghosts exist. Just one story. If you find one mysterious white crow it means that not all crows are black. One story that cannot be impeached or refuted, then we'll have it. Our case will be made. I think the big question is not if ghosts exist, but what is their nature. Why are they here? What is it about the universe that we have to discover?

DO YOU THINK THAT GHOSTS ARE BASICALLY HERE BECAUSE OF SOME GREAT EMOTIONAL OR TRAUMATIC EVENT?

I think in some instances that is true, but again some ghosts are just here. We bump into them. They're not aware of us. We stumble into them. I don't think one answer fits everything. A lot more work has to be done.

CHAPTER FIVE
MY STORY

A DUEL WITH SPIRITS FROM ANOTHER DIMENSION

There is no greater crime to commit than of that against a child.

Children who have been sexually abused are like nuclear bomb survivors. The trauma they undergo cannot be defined or explained with words. There is no language to describe their agony, as no words can describe what a nuclear bomb survivor goes through. There are no words to describe their horror. The fallout is lifelong, the radiation sickness, manifesting off and on as the body tries to heal...the child who has been abused suffers the same in the form of PTSD, anger, insomnia, mistrust, anxiety, depression... This is the fallout of a survivor of sexual abuse.

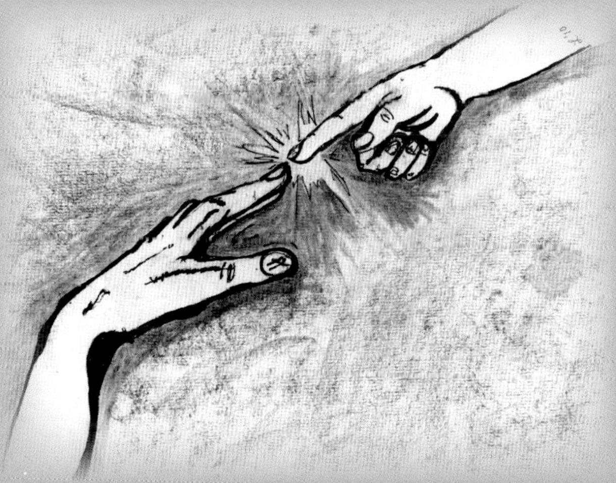

"Eternity." by *Louella Diamond*

Emotional Imprints

In Hiroshima there are shadows of human beings who were killed in the attack. Eternal. In a similar way, the trauma of being a survivor of childhood sexual abuse does not just go away with death. A child's pain transcends life and death, and this emotional imprint manifests as what we call a "ghost." This imprint is so deep that it does not end with death. Like the shadows of Hiroshima, it is embedded forever in the heart of the child who experienced it.

I believe there was a child who lived in the house I lived in who was sexually abused, and either died from the abuse or was killed. I feel that the crime was a cover-up, and went unchallenged, and that the initial contact from the boy was an attempt at reaching out to me and my neighbor at the time, psychic Louella Diamond. The boy wanted us to know what had happened, and had been waiting for the right person to come along to reveal his secret. Working together, with my relentless research and Louella's brilliant psychic sense, we were able to unlock the terrible secret of the house, and I hope release him from some of his pain.

This experience confirmed my belief in the paranormal and led to the writing of this book. It also elucidated an understanding of what is needed to understand paranormal phenomena-compassion, scientific methods, and intellect. I feel that what we think of as "ghosts" has a lot less to do with Halloween and "spooky" stuff, and much more of deep emotions. Adult ghosts are of course fascinating, but the ghosts of children are without exception one of the most fascinating creatures in the universe. They are unusually intelligent and love to play pranks. They are also extremely vulnerable. "Robbie," the name of this spirit, would sometimes try to crawl into bed with me, because of his fear. I regret that my own fear couldn't allow me to deal with that. I could not yet sleep with a ghost! I remember seeing a white swirling mist in the bed, right next to me, and felt his energy.

A Dead Phone Line

I think the story really began in August 2007 when I first moved into the house, a Victorian-style home in the west side of Santa Barbara. There was a telephone junction box attached to the outside of the house. I had to plug a jack into this box to start new phone service in my room. The phone worked for a few days. Then a few days later, I tried to make a phone call; there was nothing but static. What could have happened? When I called the phone company, they told me that someone had opened the box and unplugged the jack (and they had known my name and were able to differentiate my line from the people downstairs.) At the time of course I thought it may have been a neighbor playing a prank, but in retrospect I think it was Robbie, knowing his prank-filled personality. After that, I put a lock on the telephone junction box. What follows is a diary of the events that occurred afterwards...

THE DUEL BEGINS

TUESDAY, DECEMBER 11, 2007

Something is haunting this house. It started last week when I found the light on at 2AM in the sun room. I had turned it off the night before, like I always did. Something was trying to wake me up. The other night was worse. Again I was woken up at 2AM. I turned to look at the clock on my night stand and saw a face instead. It looked like a boy, dead, his head hanging off to the side. He was pale, his eyes closed. Like he had hung himself or had been hung. Red hair? In a kind of page boy cut, with his bangs cut across. I'm not sure if there was a rope around his neck, but his eyes were closed and he looked dead, not like someone just asleep.

The next day I confirmed with my roommate that she had not turned on the light. When I told my neighbor, she told me she had seen an apparition of a boy on the second floor balcony of the house. He was opaque, and wearing a red-striped shirt that reminded her of the 1950s. "It looked like it was too small for him." I didn't tell her which room I was in (the back room) and asked her which balcony, as there were two in the house, one in the back and one in the front. "The one in the back. He was staring out towards the train tracks." It was then that I thought there actually might be a ghost in the house.

The last few days had been sleepless. Louella suggested that I speak with *them*. I also called a paranormal research group down south and asked for advice. I left a message on their machine. They called me back immediately, and were very friendly and helpful. They asked me questions about any history of mental illness, drug use, alcohol, etc. They said to call back if I wanted them to investigate this issue.

The next night I walked around the house at around 7PM, speaking to the spirit. I was very sincere and polite when I spoke to him. "I can sense that you need help, so I just wanted you to know that I'm here for you. If you need some help, just let me know." At that moment, I felt something transpire between us. I felt that the entity understood and acknowledged what I was saying. It was around this time that the Arts and Entertainment network started their new series, *Paranormal State*, which was perfect as I was trying to understand what was happening. It was also around this time that Louella had been rambling about a "man who tried to trip her." I didn't give it much thought at the time.

WEDNESDAY, DECEMBER 12, 2007. 1:26 AM

That night I heard what sounded like two voices, high pitched, in unison. Sweet, not angry. Unearthly. Human, and also inhuman. I couldn't understand the words, but could pick up their import. Somewhat innocent...the kind of sound you would hear in a sci-fi movie. It was above my bed. The sound was only for two seconds, and then it disappeared. It was somehow electronic in nature, although it was not electronic. It just felt that way. Although at that moment I was paralyzed with fear and couldn't sleep the entire night, in retrospect I felt as if the spirit was saying, "Thank you." ☺

THURSDAY, DECEMBER 13, 2007

I stayed at Louella's house. I was terrified to sleep in my own room. Not that the spirit was malevolent, I just wasn't used to sharing my room with a ghost! At 1AM, I woke up to hear the cat meowing. I fell asleep again. I had taken a tranquilizer. I looked at the clock and found that it had been set one hour late, because it read 7:40AM. I never wake up that late. I thought something was strange. Then I saw the clock was wrong. My clock had been set back an hour late! Had Robbie come over to Louella's? Maybe he was angry that I wasn't there. That's how I felt...

FRIDAY, DECEMBER 14, 2007

Friday night I slept on the couch, after taking a sleeping pill. I went to bed at 10:35PM. I didn't' hear anything that night. Was it because I told the spirit I would not help him if he woke me up at night? I had to get some sleep!

SATURDAY, DECEMBER 16, 2007

I went to T's [name protected] house and told her what was going on... She told me that she had known for years that a spirit lives on the property, or spirits. She said they move things all the time, and that she has seen orbs of light in the house. She said one time the kitchen chairs were moved across the floor. While we were talking we heard some dishes move in the kitchen. I'm not sure if that was paranormal. She is not afraid of them. I am starting to feel that way too. She said she had asked H [name protected] if anyone had died in the house before, but the answer was "no." She said the house was built in the 1940s, but that the second floor was built in 1970.

Louella came over around 8PM. She spoke to "Robbie," the name she said he responds to. She walked up the stairs, with her cane. Her right hand was shaking. I was surprised because she had told me she wasn't afraid of ghosts. Then she told me she was channeling the fear from the boy. And she said she saw something. An image of a man dragging the boy by his feet, or arms...dragging him into where? The closet? Is that where it started? She asked Robbie several times not to wake me up. She was walking back and forth from the closet to the clothes cupboard in the corner, not sure where something had happened. She said to look up "contractor" and gave me the years 1947-48. She told me that Robbie hadn't lived in the house. Before I went to bed I asked Robbie several times to not wake me during the night. I took a sleeping pill and woke up at 12 midnight, not 1AM, to the sound of the closet shaking! Was he trying to tell me that something had happened in the closet? It went on for a few seconds, then stopped. That was okay, as it was not 1AM. He had kept his promise. He had woken me up, but not as late. I know I can trust this boy now, and I need to keep my promise to him. It is so important for me to do that, for him to trust me. I really like him, actually. He is sensitive, smart, and always keeps his promise. ☺

The next morning I looked at the closet and wondered if he had died there? I had these terrible images of someone, a man, tying a rope around his neck and then killing him. Did someone hang him? Or did the man strangle him to death in the closet? Or was it suicide? This is what I have to investigate. Did the man kill him to silence him? Or did he die of strangulation? Whether it was by his own hand or not is still the question. There were pieces of white paint on the floor this morning which I put into a plastic bag. I wanted to have some kind of proof, as I knew that no one would believe me. I told Robbie that I needed to sleep that night to do the research the next day, and he was extremely quiet. No disturbances that night. ☺

MY DAY AT THE LIBRARY

MONDAY, DECEMBER 17, 2007. LATE AFTERNOON

I went upstairs to the reference desk and asked to see the Santa Barbara City Directories from 1900. I looked up information for my address and found that mainly single men had lived there from the year that it was built. Then in 1940, a man named Mr. Evile moved in. He moved between 1947 and 1948. Louella had seen the year 1948 and a contractor. I found out that Mr. Evile was a contractor and moved in 1948. Why did he move? And where did he move to? I felt a chill run through me when I looked for his next address in the directory, to see where he had moved to...and yet was not surprised when I found out that it was the same street where my roommate had lived. I knew we were all connected in some way to what had happened in the house. I spent six hours at the library, looking through the directories and finding some of them missing. I made copies and came home. I remember walking into my room and seeing the curtain move. There was absolutely no wind in the room. When I walked towards the curtain it moved, like whoever was standing there backed into the corner as I approached them.

TUESDAY, DECEMBER 18, 2007

It poured rain during the trolley ride for my work. As I was riding around in the wet trolley, I thought of poor Robbie at home, not being able to see any of the Christmas lights. I was happy to get home to him. Nothing unusual happened that night. It made sense, as he had no reason to wake me up, as we are on the verge of cracking this case. I talked to Louella today and she told me that old man Mr. Evile was a mean SOB. She had never met him, but had heard stories that he was a pedophile, rapist, and evil person. She thinks she saw his ghost who tried to trip her. He looked like an old man. Is he trying to prevent us from solving the case? She also told me she sees Robbie lying on his back, staring at a few stars in a forest of evergreen. Is that where he is buried?

Today I went to the library and researched the microfiche for two hours to see if there were any missing children reports for December 1947, but couldn't find anything. I was also going through them quickly as I was tired. I remember I went to the Hall of Records to get information on the house and who had lived there and if anyone had died there...I had to go to a few different windows, but didn't get any information. The best place was the library.

Last night I heard something around 2:30AM. The door was slightly open, as I leave it open at night these days. I think Robbie was walking around the kitchen because I heard footsteps; the cat, and also a kitchen cabinet opening or closing. Then I felt such a strong presence by my bed and also saw something white by my bed. Maybe an outline...

THURSDAY, DECEMBER 20TH, 2007

I asked my roommate if it was her last night and she said she woke up at 3AM but didn't get up. It must have been Robbie... This morning I called the Santa Barbara genealogical society and they gave me some information.

FRIDAY, DECEMBER 21ST, 2007

I just remember last week turning off the light and the chill that filled the room. Not cold, but an icy feeling. Such fear I have never felt in the room. Not mine, but Robbie's fear. I just remembered how Louella felt nauseated after she spoke to Robbie. Last night I called the paranormal research group down south. The woman took down some information about Mr. Evile, etc. She mentioned that one of the investigators was also a crime specialist, which was good. After all, a crime had been committed, and what better combination, than that of a criminal investigator and paranormal expert? ☺

Robbie's crime had never been solved. I didn't sleep well last night. I got up at 1AM and took some Valerian. I didn't hear anything strange last night.

SATURDAY DECEMBER 22ND, 2007

I bought Robbie a Christmas present, a toy train. Louella had told me in the beginning of December about a man who had tried to trip her, and I couldn't understand what she was talking about. I just talked to her, and she told me about the ghost, who looked about ninety-four, who tried to trip her. He was wearing overalls, pockmarked, and had aging white skin. I think it might have been Mr. Evile. She felt he was a malevolent spirit. She told him to stay away from next door, meaning me. I need to get his picture. Since we knew who the person was, and that this person was quite famous in Santa Barbara, I went to the library and got a book with his picture in it; then I showed it to Louella. There were three men in the picture. I didn't tell her the names. She pointed to the man, which was a photo of Mr. Evile as a child, and said, "I feel something evil emanating from this one." I was surprised, as the boy had such a nice smile and looked so charming in his overalls.

ROBBIE'S STORY

SUNDAY DECEMBER 23, 2007

Last night was the most intense session ever. Louella was actually channeling Robbie's spirit. She came over last night around 7:30PM. She was in pain from her MS. It was so intense and so real. I could see the images of what had happened. She started off by asking him a few questions. "Is your name Robbie?"

"That's close enough. I don't know where I was buried."

He started off by saying that the old man would make him feel uncomfortable when he was in the swimming pool. Diving off a board. The old man would watch him. He talked about a little boy who had been molested, another boy in the neighborhood. His parents didn't believe him. They moved away. The boy felt ashamed. For some reason, he used to come to Mr. Evile's house and hide in the room. And then he found the room that Mr. Evile used to keep his boys. Pictures of little boys butts, photos, on the wall. A handmade bed. Toys.

His dad pumped gas. Did Mr. Evile own the gas station?

He went missing. Mr. Evile locked him in the attic. There was a window. The police came over to question, but Mr. Evile made up a lie.

"I was in the attic window but they couldn't see me; why didn't they look harder? Why didn't my mom look harder?"

Was he handcuffed and couldn't get to the window? He was so close to the window but couldn't reach it. Was he looking out the window at his parents?

Did Mr. Evile break his legs? "I was still alive when he thought I was dead."

Beyond the yard, down a hill... Was he dragged?

There was the swish of oaks and trees.

Mr. Evile took Robbie to the area. He came back two days later. Robbie must still have been alive. How did he kill Robbie? By burying him alive??

Louella said she saw Robbie looking straight up at the stars. Did Mr. Evile break his legs so he couldn't walk?

A road at the edge of a hill.

Mr. Evile kept Robbie in the attic overnight, and then wrapped him up in brown butcher paper like a piece of meat; they used to wrap meat up like that in those days. Louella said that maybe Mr. Evile broke his legs to make him fit. Then Louella pointed out the window towards the mountains.

Mr. Evile took him out in his truck.

"I loved the Chumash Indians. We learned about them in school. I've seen quite a few Indians."

"If that man built something on a Chumash site he would lie. He lied to my mom and dad."

Mr. Evile was placing alternatives in the mind of his mother and father. Telling them that maybe a coyote or mountain lion got him. He rolled him down the hill and then came back two days later. Robbie was still alive. He molested Robbie, kept him overnight in the attic, and then took him out in the truck?

"Why didn't my mom look harder?"

He was buried within a five-seven mile radius.

"I was taught to respect the Chumash."

Mr. Evile handcuffed his leg?

Within six to nine months the house was torn down. Then rebuilt?

Mr. Evile was a rich man. The police department in Santa Barbara may have been corrupt during the 1940s.

Louella thinks that Mr. Evile broke his knees to make him fit in the brown butcher paper, just like a piece of meat.

That's all we got for tonight. He didn't want to talk about it anymore.

I forget to mention that lately I've seen a lot of spiders in this room. On the curtains, in the corner, etc.

MONDAY DECEMBER 31, 2007

The last day of the year. Very nice and sunny, looks warm outside.

I have been away for a week. I spent the night at C's [name protected] house. We watched *Poltergeist*. I could have sworn I saw an Indian standing in her living room when I woke up at 2AM. Then S told me about a dream he had had, where he felt his arm was being pulled into the wall. When he woke up he felt like it was really happening. Last night I didn't hear or really see anything, but I felt an energy passing through me in the bed, and that Robbie was sleeping with me. I felt energy or a sensation passing through me.

Louella came over in the afternoon around 4PM, and said how Robbie put his arms around her and hugged her. Did she say that Robbie loved me?

My roommate had been somewhat disturbed by all the drama, and I felt the paranormal stuff was creating a gap between us, so we asked Robbie to show her some proof that he was there. It was amazing. After she had left it must have been around 5PM that I went into her room to talk to her, and then I heard a clicking sound. I took her back into my room and found the light on!!! He had turned the light on to show her. Her reply was, "Well I didn't know that it was on before." ☹ When I told this to Louella she said, "He doesn't have to prove anything to her."

TUESDAY, JANUARY 1, 2008

New Years Day. A black spider appeared with a red body. So many spiders lately, since the paranormal stuff started happening!

WEDNESDAY, JANUARY 2, 2008

The spider is resting at the top of the ceiling now.

THURSDAY, JANUARY 3, 2008—COLD AND RAINY

It's like the rain is riveting the balcony. A sharp stream of rain can be seen from my window, through the mountains. Louella told me about a dream she had. A boy running through the woods, and a man with a flannel hunter's hat and coat chasing him with an ax. It was dark. Was this Robbie and Mr. Evile? Now she says she can also see other children involved that he molested. She said his ghost, or a "composite demon" sat on her bed the beginning of December. He was wearing a cap, overalls, and chewing on something (maybe tobacco?). She said other ghosts were sitting around her bed having cereal, and that they were scared by him. Then when she tried to stand up he stuck out his leg and tripped her. She also said about six or seven ghosts gathered around her bed the beginning of December. Were they the adult ghosts of the children who had been molested? She said he was trying to blend in with everyone else. She told him to leave and never come back, and to also not go to the house next door (my house). Then she said he just sort of faded away.

You can hear the train from this room.

SATURDAY NIGHT, AROUND 8PM, JANUARY 5, 2008

Louella came over. There was a slight rain. It was freezing from the rainstorm. Below is a transcript of her speaking to Robbie.

> *You need to stick around to help me. Tell them to hold on. They can't cross over. I can't fix what already happened. Only if they're lost. You have such a generous heart. Please, don't work hard at bringing them out. Can you please wait? We'll work together.*
>
> Images of the thousands of kids that were molested come to me.
>
> *You can't bring all of them up.*
>
> He was opening up these floodgates. And then I saw this restaurant. This 1940s restaurant. A kitchen, I saw flashes. I heard the kids' voices,
>
> *You can't let them come out. Only if they're lost. Only out of their resting place, they can only come out if they're lost.*
>
> They were molested by Mr. Evile, but not killed by him. He wants to raise them above their graves and talk. He's not here, I saw the gate closing.

Later she talked about how the restaurant was being renovated. She said he was purposely trying to delay his own peace so that he could help the others. Just like a bodhisattva. Who is this boy?? Today I called X's [name protected] son. Still doing my research. He confirmed he had no younger brother who went missing. And he didn't recall anyone being missing at that time in 1947. He gave me the name of the XYZ [names protected] brothers.

TUESDAY, JANUARY 8, 2008

There isn't anything to report regarding Robbie, except that I wake up every night at around 2 or 3AM. I don't feel the jolting out of my sleep like I did before, but just waking up in general. I can't seem to sleep through the night. Louella said that maybe he was satisfied in just having someone know what had happened. After I came back from being away for a week maybe he felt like he was satisfied. She said she felt some residual paranormal element when she came over the other day.

WEDNESDAY, JANUARY 9, 2008

I didn't sleep too well last night, because around 12AM I saw something appear to fall down from the ceiling in the darkness. I can't explain it; it looked something appearing in the air, coming down towards me, and then disappearing. It scared the hell out of me, and I was very nervous. I keep waking up in the middle of the night. Cannot sleep deeply.

SATURDAY, JANUARY 12, 2008

There hasn't been much activity since I asked Robbie to let me sleep at night. A few days ago, I called X, and he told me he hadn't heard of any children who had gone missing or ran away. He did tell me the names of two boys who lived on the corner of the street which are similar to Robbie, and that would be right across the street. I tried to find information online but couldn't.

SUNDAY, JANUARY 13, 2008

My roommate left for LA on Tuesday, so I was alone. I slept on the couch for two nights. When I came back on Thursday and slept in my room, I saw and felt the sensation when I woke up in the middle of the night, in the darkness. I thought this must be Robbie. When I told him I was sick the next day and needed to sleep, it didn't happen again. I also called the Santa Barbara Historical Society on Thursday and confirmed that Robbie H. is still alive or was in 1970 from his father's obituary, so that means he isn't the Robbie we are thinking of.

SUNDAY, JANUARY 20, 2008

Louella was very sick this evening, but she came over to see if she could reach Robbie. She asked him his last name. She pronounced it "Sla. Sla. Slatty? Come on Robbie." Her signal was very weak. A very unusual name. Like a foreign name. Like a Jewish name. "Are you Jewish or Mexican?" He didn't answer. She pronounced it "Sloby. 1700 Sola. St. Louis, that's where he's from? I'm wary of that because he lived near a pine tree. I'm considering that. St. Louis is what I come up with. San Luis Obispo? The words sound like St. Louis. He was teased in school. A back yard...pine trees. Mr. Evile didn't see anything wrong with molestation. Father to son, man to man. "I'm sorry Robbie, there's nothing to be ashamed of. He became unconscious. And he, Mr. Evile, did him one last time, and I don't want to see what happened next. Robbie or Ronnie Slater or St. Louis." It was amazing that when I looked up in the Santa Barbara Directory to see if I could find a name similar to that, I found a "Robert Slxxxy" on the same street!

Last night, Sunday, I heard the sound of something that sounded like the voices of children, at different times during the dead of night. I woke up again. More than one voice. I told Robbie last night that Louella was coming over, so did he call his friends over to see her?

WEDNESDAY, JANUARY 23, 2008

Again I saw the swirling white around my head and felt it was Robbie.

THURSDAY, JANUARY 24, 2008

When I came home yesterday I actually had a message from the woman from the paranormal research society, but the light wasn't blinking. Does this mean that Robbie had played the message back so that I wouldn't know she had called? Was he bored and playing pranks again? In all the time I had this answering machine, I have never missed any messages. Could it be that Mr. Evile didn't want the investigators and police to know of his crime, and so he erased the message to disturb contact between myself and them?

I called *XYZ* to get info on *Slxxxly*, but they didn't remember anything.

PARANORMAL JUSTICE

SATURDAY, JANUARY 26, 2008

The paranormal research group came on Friday around 8:40PM. The woman called first to say they had stopped at a restaurant and were on their way. Two men and two women. They kept walking down the stairway with their EMF detectors. One of them wore his police badge and plastic name ID. It was perfect, because finally justice was being brought to Robbie. He brought a cooler and dumped the ice in the sink. They brought bottled water and four containers of applesauce. Tons of equipment. The four way remote TC. Infrared cameras. They kept walking around taking EMF readings. They set up digital recorders everywhere. I asked them to take their shoes off and they did so immediately. Lots of white cable and the orange things that help unroll it. They kept going into my room, sitting down and talking with Robbie. They would close the door; sometimes go in pairs, sometimes alone. Checking out the closet. They put a ball and doughnut on the kitchen table for Robbie to move, but he never did. They asked me to ask Robbie to interact with them. They were very nice people. My roommate stayed in her room the entire time.☺ They left at 1AM. One of the women kept saying that her batteries were going dead. Was that because the ghosts were trying to drain her with their energy? They came perfectly equipped and organized with their coolers and equipment. Digital recorders. EMF meters. No motion detectors.

SUNDAY JANUARY 27, 2008

"Robbie there are a bunch of toys here for you. I have some questions to help you get home, get back to your family."

1. How old are you?
2. Is your name Robbie?
3. Did you live next door to Mr. Evile?
4. Did he kill you?
5. Is your body buried here?
6. Did your parents report you as missing?
7. Did the police ever come to investigate?
8. Did you live on the same street as the man who hurt you?
9. What was your father's name?
10. Where were you born?
11. What was the name of your school?
12. What was the name of the pool?
13. Do you have any brothers or sisters? What are their names?
14. Did you touch my answering machine yesterday?

"You need to be reunited with them."

Sometimes Louella would rear back as if she had been hit. She always stands up when she does her reading.

> I want to help you cross over. Robbie Slxxxly? I'm confused. Talk to me, talk to the medium. I saw him outside the window. Come in. Come in a little bit? He came inside. Another voice (Hi Bobby?) He's acting different. He went back outside the window (can't understand.) I see an album of records and the toilet. Why are you holding up a record? Are you talking about the construction site? He broke the record at home and then ran out to hide in the construction site (because his parents would be angry?) I heard, "uh oh." (Because he broke the record?) Red mountain. Squeezing. Squeeze. There's a wine in the 60s. That might have been the catalyst, all the sh-- that went on at home. I see pine trees and blood? I believe he was sodomized once more before he died. He lost consciousness. He was dying. He didn't understand. His whole body was numb. Maybe his spinal cord was broken. Right before he died he got real scared. He knew he was dying, but didn't know how.

FRIDAY, FEBRUARY 1, 2008

Today I had lunch with J from work, and she shared the experience of her husband passing away, and the paranormal experience afterwards. She said three days after he died the music suddenly went on in a music box, as well as the radio in her kitchen. She said her husband had always loved electronics. This went on for about six months. Then in September she received a text message on the one year anniversary of his death on her cell phone. It said, "I love you." When she tried to investigate the source of the call she couldn't find any data. Then she found a draft he had written while he was still alive, that had been sent that day! After that the activity stopped. She said she isn't lonely, because she told him it was okay to leave. Then I thought this was maybe J's gift to me, as maybe it would be good if I told Robbie that it's okay for him to leave as well. Maybe he wouldn't leave unless he knew it's okay with me.

Sometimes at night when I put my hand up in the air I can feel the energy swirling around me.

FRIDAY, FEBRUARY 8, 2008

Last night was really scary. I heard from the paranormal research society that there were about fifteen EVPs on the tape, of about five different ghosts. I was upset about this, and couldn't sleep all night, knowing they were here, but hopefully not all in my room. This explains all the orbs that T was talking about.

THURSDAY, FEBRUARY 14, 2008

Today I received the CD package from C, but I'm a bit nervous to put it on at night. I have just listened to them. They don't seem to be a very happy bunch of spirits. I am not really afraid of them. On the contrary, I have sympathy for them and want to help them. At first I thought that their talk was unrelated to us, but now I think they are very intelligent and speaking to us. They obviously didn't want the team here. Is that why my answering machine message was on the blink that one day? Why don't they want anyone here? And then to say "I am him." Are they trying to fool us about Robbie? The only thing to do is to ask more questions. Ask their names and what happened. Why are there a mixture of spirits? And are they different voices? Some whispers, some not. A lot of the talk has negative connotations. "Hate" and "f--k" and "leave" and "go." "I'm not crazy." They definitely don't want Louella around. They seem very weak and not able to do much. Most of the talk appears to be related to our conversation except for maybe "I'm not crazy," and the woman humming. Are we experiencing a parallel universe? Where our present is their past or their present? I am thinking of the EVP that C picked up at a hotel where a woman was saying, "Please don't kill me," etc., and then found out there was a murder there.

MONDAY, MARCH 10, 2008

I heard the VCR go on last night—about 2:30AM. This morning I found the tape pushed in. Sometime in early March, I contacted the spirit in my room. Around 11PM at night. I had bought a digital tape recorder at Circuit City and was playing around with it. This was after the investigators had left. They had suggested to me that I buy one and try to contact the spirits myself. I spoke into the recorder and asked them to not come into the sun room. I spoke very seriously and respectfully to them, stating my wishes, and I could sense something listening to me. Then I said, "Good night." Imagine my shock when I played the recorder back and heard a voice slowly say, "Good night." At the end there was a little laugh, which was chilling. Louella felt that it was Mr. Evile, and that he had been trying to scare me.

FRIDAY, MARCH 28, 2008

Today I found a message on my answering machine from S. She called around 11:30AM. The first part of the message was normal and clear, but at the end I could hear some strange sounds. At first I thought it might be her cell phone still on in her purse, but after listening to it, I was sure that it was an EVP; the ghost had left a message on my answering machine! Like someone saying "goodbye" and "I repeat." When I played the message back on the computer, and listened with headphones, I could make out "Goodbye S" (her name) and "I repeat." Clearly. After listening to it for about thirty times with headphones on the digital wave player on the computer.

SATURDAY, MAY 10, 2008

Louella came over last week or the week before, I can't remember now. I asked her because T, the woman downstairs said that she had heard someone stomping or walking around in the sun room at 3:30AM a few weeks ago. That freaked me out. Around the same time I met a girl at school who told me about the significance of the northeastern direction, and that this was the path for evil spirits to enter. I went home and checked the sun room and it was that direction. I borrowed a *feng shui* compass from T and set it in the room, then I asked Louella to come over and banish the spirit from the sun room. Since then we haven't heard anything. I also tried contacting the spirit in my room, but there has been no response.

SATURDAY, MAY 31, 2008

I was up at 3AM the other night and heard the birds singing.

SUNDAY, JUNE 1, 2008

I called up Louella and she told me that Mr. Evile was right behind her last night when she was making cookies. She turned around and he was standing behind her wearing a blue apron, the kind they use to shoe horses, a blacksmith's apron. She said he was watching her make cookies. She said that maybe he used cookies to lure little boys. I was laughing so hard I was crying. I needed that.

FRIDAY, JUNE 13, 2008

Last night something appeared to me out of the darkness. Like something coming towards me, a ball maybe? Right next to my bed. It happened before, above my ceiling. I was not really scared and just went to sleep.

SUNDAY, JUNE 15, 2008

Louella didn't look too good last night. She is having seizures. She said that voices were beckoning to her, calling her name. Whispers. Could these be the ghosts, or Mr. Evile, seducing her to the other side?

MONDAY, JUNE 16, 2008

Yesterday T told me that her psychic friend downstairs, C, had seen a ghost, a woman in a black dress. She said after she saw the woman, the mirror in the room fogged up for a moment, and then shattered, and then something scurried away. She also said she woke up at 3:30AM because she could hear chairs being dragged around in the sun room. She said they can hear sounds in the kitchen, and also that her dogs freeze up and suddenly look up at something in the air, trembling, as if someone were standing there. She said sometimes the dogs stand up on their hind feet, as if someone were offering them food. Last night I could hear a kind of thumping in my room around 2AM.

SATURDAY, JUNE 21, 2008

Summer clouds today, because it was so HOT. Over 100 degrees.

Louella's story of Mr. Evile:

> There was a cartoon one time; it was a baker, and he had his hat and his apron on; he saw a mouse, and he turned around and he screamed. He was kind of chubby with a chef hat; but the way he ran, like he was kind of pigeon toed; like he was lumbering, moving forward. Shift to the right, and shift to the left, and lumber down; that's how Mr. Evile was moving, and his hands were doing the 1920s thing, when you put your hand in the hair and shake it. And I've never heard a ghost scream like that; HE was scared. By the time he got to the door he was about gone, faded away, and his apron was untied, and it flew to the right, and flew to the left; he was so afraid of me! He walked like he had deformed legs, but he didn't. But he did seem very curious; I don't think that was his motive for coming over, but he was mesmerized by me making cookies. It was close to midnight when I saw him. When I went to his face it was like going through somebody who was made of light, like a hologram. In the bedroom he tried to trip me. He was sitting on my left, on the bed. I had seen his face, his outline before. Robbie had shown him to me in the visions. I met Robbie about six months before you moved in, or maybe a year. I could feel him saying, "Help me." It was almost like, "You're gonna be here one day to play with me." I could feel him saying, "I'll see you when it's right," and I saw white wisps, but never as clear like that, like when I saw him on the balcony.
>
> Robbie's eyes—he was so alone, and so afraid. He died of injury from his molestation and exposure. Mr. Evile loved Robbie in a sick way and kept him prisoner for his pleasure. His parents were not nice people. They were cold hearted. They were extremely poor. He grew about three inches. He didn't have stamina; he was so unhealthy and malnourished. I believe he died, I wanna say 1948; it comes to me; maybe a little bit going into 1949. It would have been the next cold period…
>
> Mr. Evile raped Robbie, and he died from the hemorrhaging. He bled to death. Did he try and run away from Mr. Evile? Did he die in the woods? He was a boy of about nine years old. Mr. Evile wore a blue

chambray shirt, work shoes, overalls, and had a huge bumpy nose. I was making cookies in the early morning and felt a presence.

Louella turned around and "bumped into this nose."

That had to be something from the underworld, it was so ugly. He was wearing a blacksmith apron.

She said that he was watching her intensely, and seemed to be genuinely interested in what she was doing, and making cookies. She said that he was just as scared as she was and backed away, and then dissipated. She said that she felt that he thought that she couldn't see him. Mr. Evile first appeared in December 2007. Louella had told me before I told her about the spirit in my house, about a man who had tried to trip her, someone she had never seen before. I had no idea who she was talking about. I didn't know it was a ghost, and that she was talking about Mr. Evile. She just said a man had come into her bedroom and tried to mingle with the other ghosts, a new ghost she had never seen before. He sat on the bed and then stuck his leg out and tried to trip her when she stood up, and his leg went right through her. He appeared in December 2007, right when this whole thing came out. I feel that he was trying to prevent us from figuring out what had happened. He saw what was happening in my house, and then came over to Louella's to stop her. That would explain why the ghosts told her to get out and said "no" when she was talking about the rape. See EVPs that follow.

EVP Report from January 26, 2007

1. "Go."

This was said when we were sitting in the dining room—cannot ascertain if this is male or female.

2. "I love this, love this."

From digital tape recorder set on the fireplace mantle—a male, and I believe this is Mr. Evile, who was watching the investigation, and seemed to enjoy it!

3. "No."
Cannot ascertain if this is male or female—this was said right after Louella said, "I feel that he sodomized this child."

4. "Hate for"
From digital tape recorder set on the fireplace mantle—cannot ascertain if this is male or female.

5. "No."
From digital tape recorder set on the fireplace mantle—a male and I believe this is Mr. Evile. This was said when Louella was saying, "Slatter, Slaby, Slattey—that's pretty close."

6. "Leave, go."
This from where we were sitting at the dining room table, engaged in conversation. I believe directed especially towards Louella.

7. "Wow."
This from where we were sitting at the dining room table engaged in conversation.

8. "Get out."
This from where we were sitting at the dining room table, engaged in conversation.

9. "No—GO."
This was said after a team member, who was addressing Louella and her psychic evidence, said, "Definitely, if you come up with anything else, feel free to..." and Louella said, "I have a lot of things?" From this comment it's clear that Louella was not welcome there, nor was the team, as the spirits knew we were onto to them.

10. "___ _____ is my hobby. Yeah!"
I have listened to this about 100 times, yet cannot pick up the first two words. "is my hobby" is clear, as is the, "Yeah." This sounds like a woman, African American.

11. "Hi."

This was in response to the investigator asking, "She says that you've turned the light out on the deck. Can you turn on the light again?"

12."What the f--k?"
Disembodied voice on sun deck using profanity. We heard a voice in the background say this in response to one of the investigators joking around to another one,"If we smell something funny we'll know you're here." Then after the profanity, the investigator making the comment, "Watch your voice around the little children around here." Meaning he had thought the other investigator had said, "What the f--k?" when he had not.

13. "I am him."
From digital tape recorder set on the fireplace mantle—a male, and I believe this is Mr. Evile, who was watching the investigation.

EVP REPORT FROM EARLY MARCH

1. "Good night."
This was in my room, after I had said, "Good night."

POSTSCRIPT—THE DUEL CONTINUES

FRIDAY, OCTOBER 1ST, 2010

THE RETURN OF MR. EVILE: LOUELLA'S EXPERIENCE

I just had a very, very strong sense that somebody was in the room. I kept looking to the chair that my mother sits in and I would talk to her; the air was just thick with another person. This started around 8:30 in the morning on Friday. That went on for a while, and I was drinking my coffee and I kept hearing things. I went into the room and was talking to somebody like someone was there. I didn't even consider it on a psychic or intuitive level, you know, it was just like, you know when somebody's home and you hear them rattling around in the house, and things would be dropping. I would hear the scrape and stuff, and I was trying to get my materials ready to do some sketching, and some of my stuff had fallen, and I felt a light push on my tailbone. Just so I would fall forward; this was right outside my door as I was going from my room to the couch. Things had been falling all day from my room; I was hearing things fall, and things were falling in the living room, and it was scaring my dog, she wanted to go back into my mom's room. It sounded like dishes were falling, forks, spoons, magazines, pens, caps of pens, they all sounded different. Then I got mad and said, "Who's here? Daddy? If it's you, I know you will let me know by your feelings, and that you will come over and give me the warmth of your love, and if it's not Father, then it's Mr. Evile;" (Louella's dad had died a year earlier). But I felt that it was just the parts of his soul that were strong enough to break through from the walls of the other side. And I knew those emotions were his so called "love" for Robbie, and his fear of his name being printed in the book.

MAGAZINES IN THE AIR

After all this, the biggest thing that happened was I was in my room getting some things and I saw two magazines being raised up off my bed, and I said, "Oh my god, what the hell is that?"

They were picked up by the corner of the magazines, and they were lifted off of the bed, straight up, hanging. Thin air. Some entity had picked up two magazines and they were lying flat, and they were hanging. Above the bed. They weren't touching the bed. And they stood there. The magazines just stood there.

It was very feeble; It just made me think that he's not all here; just his strong emotions coming out. He kept pointing to his head; one time he pointed to his mouth. It made me think that only the strongest part that had became an entity had come (instead of a ghost.) And then it was like someone tossed them at me, and one of them hit me. And that's when I decided I needed to take care of this. We're talking early afternoon now. I've seen things lifted in the air, just to fall down, like maybe kinetic energy. I've never seen anything move. It's like fingers were holding them, and they tossed them, and there wasn't a lot of power because they weren't being held by the fists, but by the fingers. Little fingers, and they were tossed at me. And I saw them being tossed at me. At about my waist, and the bottom of the magazine hit my tailbone. The other one barely missed me.

At that point I said, "Father if it's you, you will come to me." And I knew it wasn't dad; and then I saw what looked like the outline of a ghost. I saw a white outline of a figure, standing behind a chrome shelving unit that he hid behind, so I couldn't reach him. And this was when he told me why he was there, and why he was sabotaging.

Missing Glasses

He also hid all my glasses, and when I found them, that's another story, that was weird. I found them one by one in bizarre places where they should have been broken. The car—you open the door, the opening where you slam the door... It was inside—you know, when you open the door-that opening when you slam the door? Right there, the glasses were there. They should have been smashed; so when I opened the door to get to the back seat there were a pair of glasses there. There is no way the glasses could be there without being smashed. They were inside the part of the metal in the car where the door would crush them when it closed. Someone must have placed them there after I opened the door in a few seconds because when I opened the door, if the glasses were there when I opened the door they would have been smashed, too. So the glasses had to have been put there after I opened the door, which means someone put them there within two or three seconds after I opened the door—with me there to see them.

A Deep Hatred, Strong Pride, Shallow "Love"

So, anyway, here I am talking to this person. It's not completely Mr. Evile. He is not talking, but using me to talk to me inside.

No, no, no, I did not; you're wrong about me, I loved that boy, and the way you talk, you make me out to be a monster; I loved him. I kept him in a place where he could sleep, and I fed him and you make it sound like I was a bad man. I looked for him, I could not find him.

And I told him that I accepted it, that I accepted that he loved the boy. I said, "I do not understand," but I believe that is what he believed. That was one thing. The other thing was,

You're gonna ruin my family. My family must not be marred. I have a big name in this town.

And I said, "I know, don't' worry, she's not gonna put your name in the book; no one is gonna know it's you." Then I felt that there was something else; that he was looking for Robbie, and that I felt he would try and come back and follow me and hang around and I told him, "I didn't know where Robbie is, but Robbie has been reunited with his family." I said, "You'll never see that boy again, and you need to accept that; don't bring your entity here again; don't use me to find him." I told him, "You will never see him again, so get that through your head; he's gone and you will never see that boy ever, ever again." I told him to go back to Mr. Evile and stay together as one. "You are not to be fragmented again; don't ever come back here." I said, "Are you ready to go?" And he put his finger on his head. And I said, "Go." And he left. He was fragmented in that it wasn't all of Mr. Evile; it was only his love and his fear; I couldn't reach the mind of him. It was only those emotions that could cross over; he had fragmented himself; that's what my thought is.

This entity that I talked to was like... the only thing on his mind was "my good name" and "I loved Robbie." He came only for that. It was like he sent a little pigeon from his soul to send a message to me; it wasn't completely him, it was a part of him, that was so strong, emotions—the deep dark-most deep and powerful emotions, fear, love, hate—that were able to cross over. An entity is a part of a ghost; the ghost is that part of the soul of the person that will not leave the realm of the living because of unfinished business. The entity is the strongest, most harmful part of the ghost. A form of energy.

EVP—Mr. Evile breathed on her. He is obsessed with the hunt of finding him.

It was only part of him, part of his emotions; he didn't understand anything. I said, "You kept Robbie there," and he was like—what?? I kept him there? What? 1948-What? "I loved that boy and you told me I didn't, and I loved that boy." And then he was worried about his name. "You can't use my name." He just came as a mission for those two things.

There were other things that happened; it was such a strange morning; I felt like he was so close to me and following me. It was only these strong emotions. He said after Robbie ran away, he looked for him, but he couldn't find him. Robbie ran away.

What I called upon was not fully him; it didn't have a full consciousness.

His power and hatred of us… Robbie got loose and ran away; he got into a woody part that wasn't developed, and he put the leaves over him to keep him warm, and he fell asleep and then when he woke up, he could see his own body, and when he woke up he was dead; he died from the infection on top of the exposure; Mr. Evile kept him upstairs in the house; about ten months; he had a place for him. It was about ten months he was able to pull it off.

It was some kind of room. He actually made the room; like a lean to. I can see it; he made it very hastily; he didn't want Robbie to yell out. And you're not supposed to cry out because he thinks you're enjoying it; he had to play the part; he thought that Mr. Evile would go crazy and kill him. Robbie was gone in '48. Mr. Evile thought the police would find him and he didn't want to get busted; he was just selfish, trying to save his ass. He loved Robbie like child molesters do. He's a stone-cold child molester who covered his tracks. He's a sick man; and he's a criminal man. But in his own sickness that's what he thinks. He was truly looking for him, but when he realized he couldn't find him, he cleaned up his sh-- and left; he thought of no one but himself.

I told him, "Your name will not be in the book. Now you go and don't come back; are we clear?" And he pointed to his head and shook his head. And all I saw was a white outline. And after that, no problem; and twenty minutes to an hour later, I found my glasses, one by one. They were all hidden in the weirdest places.

The glasses—I found them on top of the bed, and then found the next pair on the bottom of a little white tray; I never touch this. It was filled with stuff; they would have been on top, not the bottom, if I had put them there. I found another pair, right on the floor, in front of the house. And the car—I opened the door and they were in the well of the door; when I opened the door he must have put them in a split second; they should have been broken.

SPIRITLAND HAIKU

Spirits sea sky sun...
Souls making their journey to...
Point Conceptión...

A beach on the Central Coast. *Courtesy of David Namminga.*

ENDNOTES AND SELECTED BIBLIOGRAPHY

[1]NASA. www.nasa.gov/. Accessed May 2011.

[2] The Chumash People. Wikipedia. http://en.wikipedia.org/wiki/Chumash_people. Accessed May 2010.

[3] Chief Seattle's Famous Speech to President Franklin Pierce http://www.childrenoftheearth.org/chief_seattle.htm. Accessed April 2010.

[4, 5] Haley, Brian D., University of California, Riverside. Wilcoxon, Larry L. "Point Conceptión and the Chumash Land of the Dead: Revisions from Harrington's Notes." Journal of California and Great Basin Anthropology, 21(2). [3]The PapCTS of John P. Harrington, Volume III: Southern California/Basin.1. (Harrington, 1986:R1.07, Fr.233-234.) Published by the University of California. URL: http://escholarship.org/uc/item/4v68n5gk?query=Chumash#page-9. Accessed April 2010.

[6] Wikipedia. "Santa Barbara Mission." http://en.wikipedia.org/wiki/Mission_Santa_Barbara. Accessed April 2010.

[7] *Santa Barbara Missions You've Never Seen.* Neal Graffy http://www.edhat.com/site/tidbit.cfm?id=3446. Accessed August 2010.

[8] http://missions.bgmm.com/barbara.htm. Accessed April 2010.

[9] http://www.californiamissions.com. Accessed April 2010.

[10] *The Ghosts of Mission Santa Barbara.* http://www.youtube.com/watch?v=dBOJ2L_nDUw. Accessed April 2010.

[11] *The Santa Barbara Morning Press* February 28th, 1896.

[12] *The Ghosts of the California Missions. Richard Senate.* http://www.ghostvillage.com. Accessed April 2010.

[13] Bartoy, Kevin. Erlandson, Jon M. University of Oregon, Eugene. Cabrillo, The Chumash, and Old World diseases. Journal of California and Great Basin Anthropology. Vol. 17, No. 2, pp. 153-173 (1995). Published by the University of California. UC Merced Library, UC Merced. URL: http://escholarship.org/uc/item/3k52f936#. Accessed April 2010.

[14] *The Ghosts of the California Missions* by *Richard Senate.* http://www.ghostvillage.com. Accessed May 2010.

[15] http://www.syvnews.com/articles/2010/04/01/opinion/op2.txt.

[16] *Retrocognition at Mission La Purisima Conceptión. Richard Senate*. http://www.ghostvillage.com. Accessed May 2010.

[17] The Gaviota Conservancy. http://www.gaviotacoastconservancy.org. Accessed August 2010.

[18] Gaviota Beach. http://www.beachcalifornia.com. Accessed August 2010.

[19] The History of Cold Springs Tavern. http://www.coldspringtavern.com/history.html. Accessed August 2010.

[20] Wikipedia. "Rancho Las Cruces." http://en.wikipedia.org/wiki/Rancho_Las_Cruces. Accessed August 2010.

[21] A History of the Las Cruces Adobe. Barry N. Zarakov. *Noticias.* Santa Barbara Historical Museum. 1976. http://www.sbcordero.net/Zarakov.pdf. Accessed August 2010.

[22] http://www.militarymuseum.org/Ellwood.html. Accessed August 2010.

[23] http://en.wikiquote.org/wiki/Hamlet. Accessed May 2010.

[24] *The Santa Barbara Daily Press* February 25th, 1873."Captured Dream-A Brief History of the Lobero Theater." Otis Wickenhaeuser.

[25] La Cumbre Junior High School. http://www.sbsdk12.org. Accessed May 2010.

[26] *The Spirit of the Big Yellow House—A History of Summerland's Founding Family*. Rod Lathim.

[27] "Santa Maria Inn steeped in Central Coast history." May 6, 2007. http://www.santamariatimes.com. Accessed May 2010.

[28] Wikipedia. "Madame Butterfly." http://en.wikipedia.org/wiki/Madama_Butterfly. Accessed August 2010.

[29] *'Más allá' de Ventura*. *Ventura County Star*. http://www.vcstar.com. Accessed July 2010.

[30, 31] *The Ghosts and Legends of the Olivas Adobe*. Richard Senate.

[32] http://articles.latimes.com/1997-01-02/entertainment/ca-14827_1_ventura-city-hall. Accessed August 2010.

[33] *The Ghosts and Legends of the Olivas Adobe.* Richard Senate.

[34] "To Catch a Ghost." Matthew Singer. *The Ventura County Reporter.* July 26th, 2010.

[35] Wikipedia. "The Pierpont Inn." http://en.wikipedia.org/Pierpont Inn. Accessed June 2010.

[36] The Pieropont Inn. http://www.Pierpontinn.com. Accessed May 2010.

[37, 38, 39, 40] Script for *The Historic Haunts of High Street.* Copyright 2010 Rosemary Moffat. All rights reserved.

[41] Wikipedia. "Shangri-La." http://en.wikipedia.org/wiki/Shangri-La. Accessed August 2010.

[42] Wikipedia. "Ojai, California." http://en.wikipedia.org/wiki/Ojai,_California. Accessed August 2010.

[43] Meher Mount. http://www.mehermount.org. Accessed August 2010.

[44] http://www.unexplained-mysteries.com/column.php?id=155444. Accessed August 2010.

[45] Wikipedia. "Ectoplasms." http://en.wikipedia.org/wiki/Ectoplasm_%28paranormal%29. Accessed August 2010.

[46] The Paso Robles Inn. http://www.pasoroblesinn.com/paso_robles_history.html. Accessed May 2010.

[47] *Courtesy of The Paso Robles Inn*.

[48] Andrea Strickley, *The North County Tribune*, February 14, 2001.

[49] "Ghost story turns revamp into success story for the inn." *The Pacific Coast Business Times.* February 23-March 1st 2001. Gretchen Macchiarella.

[50] *California Hauntspitality. page 142.* Date of publication and author unknown.

[51] [52,] [53,] *20 Questions with Richard Senate.* http://www.hauntedamericatours.com/20questions/RichardSenate.htm. Accessed April 2010.

ACKNOWLEDGMENTS

I wish to thank the Buddhism of Nichiren Daishonin, which has provided the spiritual basis of my life. Nam Myoho Renge Kyo.☺

Very Special Thanks go out to paranormal researcher Richard Senate, who from the beginning provided his time and support towards the completion of this book. Thank you so much! Richard can be reached at: http://www.phantombookshop.com/.

Also Very Special Thanks to Louella Diamond, brilliant psychic, artist, and dear friend, who introduced me to the world of the paranormal, providing lots of laughter and love along the way.

Many Thanks also go out to:

Deborah Cooke for editorial assistance.

Members of the Santa Ynez Band of Chumash Indians.

La Cumbre Junior High School
http://www.sbceo.k12.ca.us/~lacumbre/

The Lobero Theatre
http://www.lobero.com

The Cold Spring Tavern
http://www.coldspringtavern.com

NASA
http://www.nasa.gov/

Rod Lathim
www.rodlathim.com

La Purisima Mission State Historic Park
http://www.lapurisimamission.org

Mission Santa Barbara
http://santabarbaramission.org/

The Pierpont Inn
http://www.pierpontinn.com/

Haskell's Designs
http://www.haskellsdesigns.com/

The Paso Robles Inn
http://www.pasoroblesinn.com/

The Glen Tavern Inn
http://www.glentavern.com/

The Olivas Adobe
http://www.olivasadobe.org/

Ventura City Hall
http://www.cityofventura.net/

The Candlelight Kitchen and Bar
http://candlelightbar.com/

The Bella Maggiore Inn
www.bellamaggioreinn.com

The Kaleidoscope Inn
http://www.kaleidoscopeinn.com/

The Fresh Mex Restaurant
http://www.freshmexco.com/

The Santa Maria Inn
http://www.santamariainn.com

Wardlow Insurance

High Street Theater
www.highstreetartscenter.com

The Secret Garden Restaurant
http://www.thesecretgardenrestaurant.com/

Bruce Hamilton

Steward

Elisabetta Lucernari

Rosemary Moffat
and the Historic Haunts of High Street in Moorpark

California State Parks and Recreation Department
http://www.parks.ca.gov/

Gaviota State Park
http://www.parks.ca.gov/?page_id=606

David Namminga
www.davidnamminga.com

Special thanks to my editor Dinah Roseberry, for her extreme patience, accessibility, and sense of humor!

Thanks to Alexander Diaz for poker game consultation.☺